Pathways of America
Lewis and Clark

by
Lynda Hatch
illustrated by Ted Warren

Cover by Ted Warren

ISBN No. 0-86653-799-6

Printing No. 98765

Good Apple
A Division of Frank Schaffer Publications, Inc.
23740 Hawthorne Boulevard
Torrance, CA 90505-5927

Dedication

To the "Neighbors on the Hill" in Eugene, Oregon, who gave me the present of *The Lewis and Clark Country* book. . .

And to my fourth grade students from Bear Creek School in Bend, Oregon, who helped me explore Lewis and Clark country–from "living history" at Fort Clatsop to Rock Fort at dusk along the Columbia River.

Introduction

Pathways of America: Lewis and Clark covers the two-year, four-month 7500-mile (12,075-kilometer) journey of Lewis and Clark. Each of the major sites along the trail is highlighted in chronological order, including detailed background information, journal quotations, memorable stories, and a bibliography. Quality activities for the students accompany each site description to teach about life along the journey, natural and cultural discoveries, geography concepts, and information about historic sites that can be visited. The activities are purposely designed in an open-ended manner with few right and wrong answers to allow students of all ages and abilities to ponder and tackle the problems.

The information is detailed to provide the teacher with a thorough, accurate background on the journey. Teachers usually don't have access to all the books that contain the information or the time to research the amount of detail that is needed for their teaching. Hopefully this book will provide that resource for the teacher. Although it is detailed, it will also be of interest to students who either read it on their own or hear the stories read aloud to them. This book attempts to cover the information accurately. As with any history, there are often differing opinions, so numerous sources were used to get the most accepted information. Notice that when journals are quoted, the spelling and punctuation are left in their original forms, although sometimes the journal translations don't agree on some details.

As they study the journey of Lewis and Clark using the resources provided in this guide, your students will become fascinated by this amazing journey, and they might even be inspired to seek adventures of their own, to enrich their lives, and contribute knowledge and understanding for all people.

Table of Contents

Notes to the Teacher

Most activities in this book are open-ended with no particular right answers, as long as correct historical facts are used. The History Time Line, however, does have exact answers.

September 23, 1806	The Lewis and Clark expedition returned to St. Louis.
September 8, 1810	The start of John Jacob Astor's fur-trading business
June 19, 1812	President Madison declared war on Great Britain.
February 17, 1820	The Senate passed the Missouri Compromise Measure.
April 17, 1824	A U.S.-Russia treaty was signed.
March 3, 1825	Congress authorized a survey to mark the Santa Fe Trail.
April 10, 1830	William Sublette led ten wagons out of St. Louis.
June 30, 1834	Congress established a Department of Indian Affairs.
September 12, 1836	Dr. Marcus Whitman reached Fort Vancouver.
May 22, 1843	The first of 1000 pioneers left Missouri, bound for Oregon.
June 15, 1846	Congress agreed to set the Oregon-British boundary.
January. 24, 1848	Gold was discovered at Sutter's Creek near Sacramento, California.
February 2, 1848	The U.S. and Mexico signed the Treaty of Guadalupe Hidalgo.
August 14, 1848	President Polk signed the Oregon Bill.
September 16, 1858	The Butterfield Overland Mail Company started its first run.
April 3, 1860	The first run of the Pony Express left St. Joseph, Missouri.
November 6, 1860	Abraham Lincoln was elected President of the United States.
April 12, 1860	The Civil War began.
October 24, 1861	The first transcontinental telegraph line was linked up.
April 9, 1865	The Civil War ended.
April 15, 1865	President Lincoln died after being shot by an assassin.
March 30, 1867	Alaska Purchase Treaty transferred Alaska to the U.S.
May 10, 1869	First U.S. transcontinental railroad was completed.
March 1, 1872	President Grant signed an act of Congress creating Yellowstone.
December 29, 1890	The last major battle between Indians and U.S. Army

Note: The term *Indian* has been used throughout the book as it was during the days of Lewis and Clark. Today, some people prefer the term *Indian*, some prefer *Native American*, and some feel either is fine. So as not to offend anyone, it is important to use the term that is most preferred in your area. Remember to avoid stereotypes and Hollywood portrayals so the students will have a richer appreciation and understanding of all peoples.

If students live near the route of the Lewis and Clark expedition or travel to the route, they should be aware of the signs that mark the trail. The Lewis and Clark Trail Commission was established by Congress in 1964. Lewis and Clark Trail signs are put up along the route at the suggestion of the commission. The following is the design of each sign:

Route of the Lewis and Clark Expedition

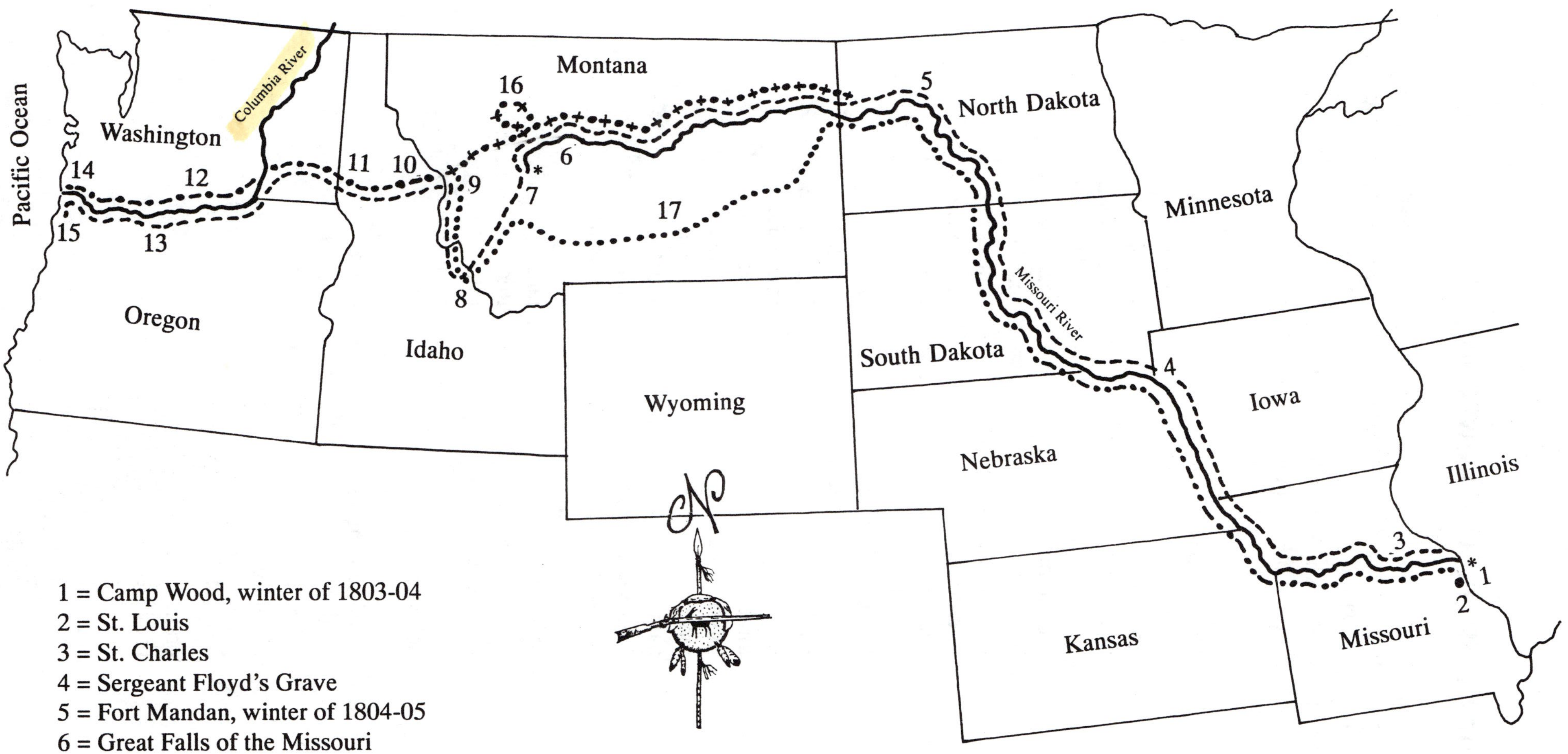

1 = Camp Wood, winter of 1803-04
2 = St. Louis
3 = St. Charles
4 = Sergeant Floyd's Grave
5 = Fort Mandan, winter of 1804-05
6 = Great Falls of the Missouri
7 = Three Forks
8 = Lemhi Pass
9 = Traveler's Rest
10 = Lolo Pass
11 = Canoe Camp
12 = Celilo Falls
13 = Long and short narrows
14 = Cape Disappointment
15 = Fort Clatsop, winter of 1805-06
16 = Marias River (loop)
17 = Pompey's Pillar

Key

** = Length of Missouri River
- - - - = Route of outward journey (1804-05)

Route of return journey (1805-06)

–·–·– = Return trip together through Oregon and Idaho
+·+·+ = Return of Lewis (through Montana)
• • • • = Return of Clark (through Montana)
–··–·· = Return together down the Missouri River following the route of the outward journey

The route of the Lewis and Clark expedition traveled through eleven of today's United States.

Preparation for Studying the Lewis and Clark Expedition

If the following words are understood, the concepts in the book will be easier. Reading history can be difficult because of words that aren't in use today. Students will enjoy the spellings and word usages of the journals from the Lewis and Clark expedition. The text was written as background information for the teacher. It is also for the students, but depending on their abilities, teachers may need to guide them through the reading.

ambassador
appendix
artery
artifacts
astronomy
awning
bison
blubber
cache
calico
caulk
centennial
chiggers
coincidence
commence
compass
confluence
conqueror
continent
court martial
cultural
current
discipline
embark
engrave
epidemic
expedition
famished
fatigue
flogging
forage
forge
frostbite
geology
geography
geyser

Great Britain/England
hardship
hominy
humane
hypothermia
Indian mound
influenza
insubordination
interpreter
keelboat
landmark
latitude/longitude
Louisiana Purchase
malaria
migrating
militia
missionaries
moccasins
navigation
Nobel Laureates
nomadic
Northwest Passage
oblique
party (group)
peace council
peace pipe
pemmican
pewter
physical features
pigment
pirogue
plantation
portage
portrait
prairie
provisions

rapids
revenge
Revolutionary War
rheumatism
rudder
scaffold
scarlet
sculpture
seaworthy
sergeant
silhouette
sloth
smallpox
Spain/Spanish
spawn (salmon)
specimens
stampede
stockade
suet
suicide
surgeon
surveying
tanning (hides)
thicket
toll
transcontinental
translate
tributary
trinket
United Nations
volcano
voyage
voyageurs
warrior
waterfowl
wound

The Dream of President Thomas Jefferson

For thousands of years, Indians lived in the Pacific Northwest of North America, but after 1700 Spanish, Russian, and British sea captains arrived to trade and claim some of the land for their countries. In 1792 Robert Gray, an American, explored and named the Columbia River. He developed a fur-trading business called the Yankee Triangle Trade. Gray bought sea otter pelts from Indians along the Northwest coast and took them to China to sell. While in China, he bought tea and other valuable goods which he later sold for a profit to the Americans. Although about one hundred Indian nations had a stronger claim to the land, Russia, Spain, Great Britain, and the United States all hoped to claim the Northwest coast and get wealthy from the fur trade.

Long before Thomas Jefferson became the third President of the United States, he was also interested in these western lands. Several times he tried unsuccessfully to send exploring expeditions, especially to the lands that lay between the Mississippi River and the Rocky Mountains. Jefferson wasn't able to send a successful expedition until after he became President in 1801. In 1802 he read about the fur trapper Alexander Mackenzie crossing Canada's Rocky Mountains to the Pacific Ocean in 1792-93. The account of this trip stirred Jefferson's imagination, but it also left him uneasy. Mackenzie's trip strengthened Great Britain's claim to the Northwest as well as opened new routes for the fur trade. Jefferson wanted an expedition from the United States to also explore these western lands. As President, he could make his dream a reality. Jefferson chose Meriwether Lewis to be his personal secretary, partly because he had already planned for him to lead an expedition to the West.

Lewis asked William Clark to be his partner. Lewis wrote to Clark, "If there is anything in this enterprise which would induce you to participate with me in its fatigues, its dangers and its honors, believe me there is no man on earth with whom I should feel an equal pleasure in sharing them as with yourself. I make this communication to you with the privity of the President, who expresses an anxious wish that you could consent to join me in this enterprise." Clark wrote back, "My friend, I join you with hand and heart." Both men were expert frontiersmen and successful in the army. Jefferson persuaded Congress to approve the expedition and to give $2500 to cover expenses. (As it turned out, the final cost was almost twenty times that amount, at $38,722.25, not counting services and materials provided by the War Department.)

Meanwhile, as Lewis was starting to make plans for the expedition, the United States government was becoming very concerned about who controlled Louisiana, this land between the Mississippi and the Rockies. Spain had been forced to give Louisiana back to France, which had lost it to them in 1763. It had been bad enough having a weak nation like Spain controlling the Louisiana country, but a strong one like France, which was led by Napoleon, could cause trouble. Jefferson worried about losing access to the Mississippi River port at New Orleans, for defense and for shipping American crops of corn, wheat, and tobacco. Jefferson sent representatives to France to try to buy New Orleans. Napoleon needed money to fight England, and he also realized he couldn't stop Americans from traveling west since they outnumbered the French in that part of the world. On April 30, 1803, Napoleon decided to sell *all* of Louisiana to the United States, not just New Orleans! This Louisiana Purchase, as it became known, was a huge piece of land that reached from the Gulf of Mexico to the upper part of today's Montana and from the Mississippi River to today's border of Montana and Idaho. The United States was able to buy the entire area for only 15 million dollars. This was an incredible bargain at only about three cents an acre. The Louisiana Purchase, which later made up all or part of fifteen future states, more than doubled the land of the young United States.

This Louisiana Purchase gave Jefferson both a reason and an opportunity to continue his dream of westward exploration. Louisiana had become part of the United States and was no longer foreign property. He was determined to find out all he could about the new territory. A survey of the new lands was critical. Because Jefferson had planned this expedition for so many years, Lewis and Clark were given detailed instructions of what to look for and what to bring back. They were to explore the area while respecting the lives of the Indians. Jefferson's orders were perhaps the most complete and humane orders ever given to explorers. Years later President John F. Kennedy recognized Jefferson's genius. At a formal White House dinner, to which he had invited America's Nobel Laureates, Kennedy gave this toast, "There hasn't been this much intellect gathered around this table since Thomas Jefferson dined alone."

Jefferson wanted to know Louisiana's geographical features, the length and location of its rivers, its potential for economic and agricultural development, the location and number of its Indian tribes, possible sites for forts and trading posts to protect future settlers, and possibilities for settlements. Jefferson was critical of the little information Mackenzie had recorded about his journey so he insisted that the Lewis and Clark expedition keep much more detailed journals. Officially Jefferson said the purpose of the mission was to do scientific and geographic research. He said nothing about America's interest in claiming the Northwest or taking away some of Canada's fur trade. He did not want other countries to recognize his plans and increase their own efforts to seize the land.

Most importantly, Jefferson wanted to find an easy water route connecting the Mississippi River with the Pacific Ocean. There were no accurate maps of the region. Jefferson thought that perhaps the Missouri, Mississippi, and the Columbia rivers might connect or be close enough together to form a "Northwest Passage" across North America. If this proved true, Americans could travel almost nonstop from St. Louis all the way to the Pacific and on to China. If such a waterway existed, the young United States would quickly become a much more powerful nation. Jefferson hoped the Lewis and Clark expedition would find this Northwest Passage and claim it for the United States.

Jefferson's directions to Lewis on June 20, 1803, were: "The object of your mission is to explore the Missouri river, & such principal stream of it, as, by it's course and communication with the waters of the Pacific ocean. . . may offer the most direct & practicable water communication across this continent."

1804 Land Claims

Debate who should claim the land west of the Mississippi River.

The map below shows which countries claimed land in 1804 that would later become the United States. These lands became the property of these countries in different ways, such as:

1. Explorers got to the land first and claimed it for their countries
2. Some were seized during war
3. Some were traded away from one country to another
4. Some were bought from one country and became property of the new country

Imagine that each of the following interested parties claims all the land west of the Mississippi River. Divide into six groups, with each group pretending to be one of the following groups. Debate which group should have all the land.

1. England
2. France
3. Indians
4. Russia
5. Spain
6. United States

Note: Obviously all of the Indians were not one big tribe. For the sake of argument, think of the claims of the Indians in *general.*

You might want to divide into seven groups and have one group pretend to be the United Nations. The United Nations was not formed until 1942, but pretend it existed in 1804. Let each of the six groups research and prepare arguments as to why *they* should get all of the land west of the Mississippi. Each group should make a poster that probably includes a map to strengthen their arguments. Then each group will come forward, show their posters, and explain why *they* should get the land. After all groups have presented their arguments, the groups can ask one another questions. After hearing all of the presentations and discussion, the United Nations will make the decision as to which group "wins."

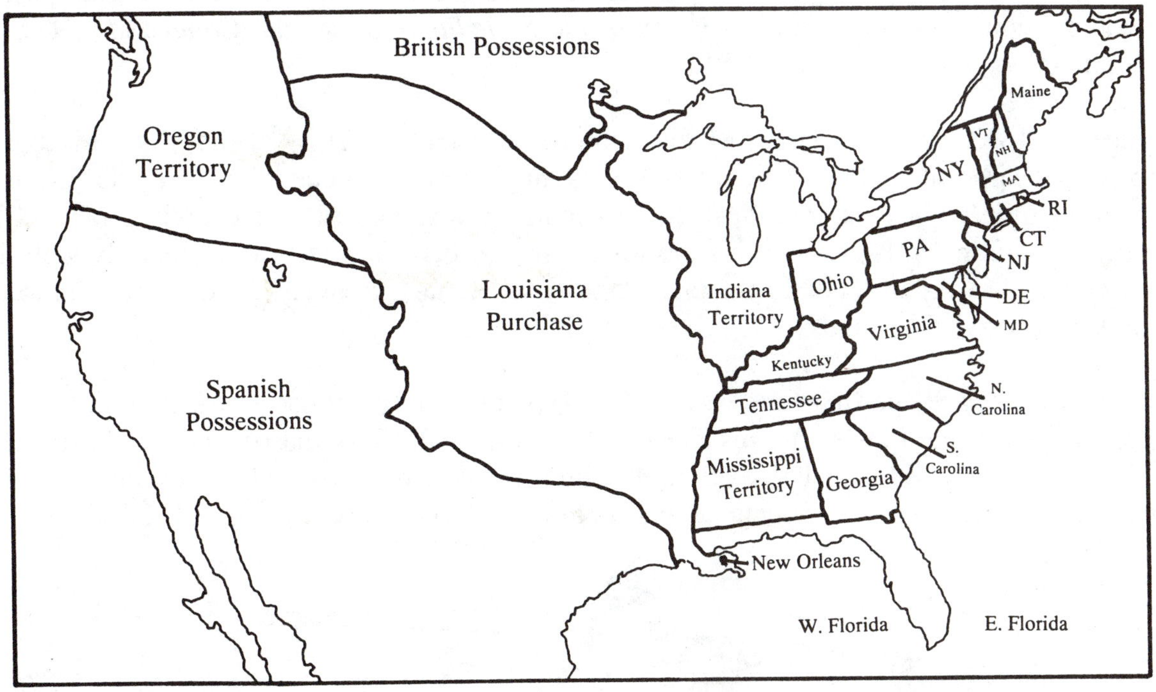

William Clark

Before the Expedition

Clark was born on August 1, 1770, in Virginia. He was one of ten children. His most famous brother was General George Rogers Clark. Like most frontier children, William Clark grew up with little schooling but knew a great deal about the woods and about Indians. He was cheerful, even-tempered, and outgoing. When he was 14, the family moved to today's Louisville, Kentucky, which was then on the edge of the American frontier. He enlisted in the militia in 1789 at age 19 and transferred to the regular army in 1791. Four years later he was put in charge of a select company of riflemen at Fort Greenville, Ohio. It was here that he met Meriwether Lewis. In 1796 Clark resigned because of financial problems at home in Kentucky. He farmed the family property until Lewis invited him to join the expedition.

After the Expedition

After being welcomed back from the expedition in Washington, D.C., with briefings, banquets, and balls, Clark became the Superintendent of Indian Affairs and Brigadier General of the territorial militia of the Louisiana Territory. He worked to keep peace among the Indians. He was liked and trusted by them. The Indians who came to St. Louis were always welcomed in his home. They called him Red Head Chief because of his red hair. He also defended the area from invasions by other countries during the War of 1812.

Clark wrote a letter to Charbonneau (one of the interpreters with the expedition) on August 20, 1806, saying, "As to your little son (my boy Pomp), you well know my fondness for him and my anxiety to take and raise him as my own child. . . ." In 1808 Charbonneau and Sacagawea arrived in St. Louis with their son. Sacagawea had a baby girl, Lizette, in August of 1812. Although historians disagree, some feel that four months later, Sacagawea died. Clark raised Pomp, Lizette, and later, Toussaint, a son of Charbonneau by his second Shoshone wife.

Clark arranged for Nicholas Biddle to rewrite the journals of Lewis and Clark, since at his death Lewis had not done any of the rewriting. Biddle did a super job and would accept no pay. The two-volume edition was called the *History of the Expedition Under the Command of Captains Lewis and Clark* and was issued in 1814.

On June 16, 1813, President James Madison appointed Clark governor of the Missouri Territory. Clark was reappointed three times. Clark was an extremely successful territorial governor, although he didn't enjoy the job. President James Monroe appointed him Superintendent of Indian Affairs again in 1821. He held this job for the rest of his life. Clark was generally well liked, but some people were upset that he wanted to treat the Indians so fairly. He did not want to force the Indians to leave their lands.

Clark married twice. The first time was to Julia Hancock, and they had five children. He named the oldest Meriwether Lewis after his friend. After Julia died, Clark married Harriet Radford, and they had two more children. Clark died in 1838 and was buried in St. Louis where his funeral procession was a mile long. At his death he was mourned by whites and Indians alike.

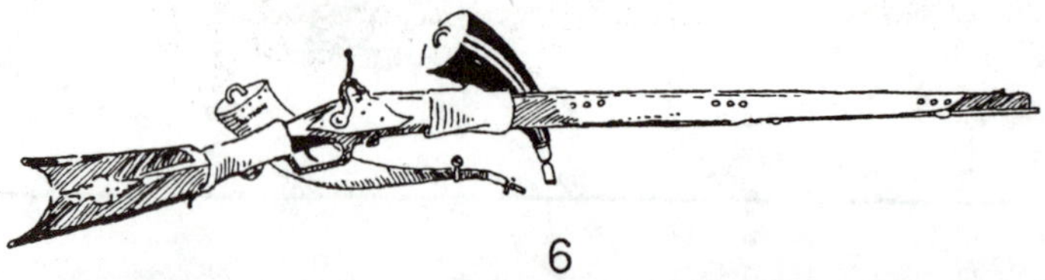

Meriwether Lewis

Before the Expedition

Lewis was born at the family's plantation in Virginia on August 18, 1774. His first name was his mother's maiden name. He was a moody boy and spent much of his time alone in the woods hunting with his dogs. His father died during the Revolutionary War when Lewis was five. His mother remarried and they lived in Georgia and Virginia. He left school at age fifteen to work the family plantation. He also spent time in the military. It was during his time at Fort Greenville, Ohio, that he met William Clark and they became friends.

Lewis was President Jefferson's private secretary from 1801-03. He shared Jefferson's dream of an overland expedition. Jefferson wrote this about him: "Capt. Lewis is brave, prudent, habituated to the woods, & familiar with Indian manners & character. He is not regularly educated, but he possesses a great mass of accurate observation on all the subjects of nature. . . ."

After the Expedition

After the expedition's return, Lewis went to Washington, D.C., where there were many banquets and awards in his honor. He was then named governor of the Louisiana Territory, the northern part of the Louisiana Purchase, with headquarters in St. Louis. There were disputes over land and mining claims. Settlers and fur trappers moved onto Indian lands, ignoring the treaties. Governor Lewis made enemies as he tried to settle land claims and keep fair trade policies with the Indians. He made matters worse by drinking too much. He was not able to write his formal report of the expedition that Jefferson had requested.

In 1809 Lewis learned that the government would not pay some of his expenses for running the Louisiana Territory. This would bring him to near bankruptcy. He left for Washington, D.C., to personally clear up the problem. Along the way, on October 10, he stopped for the night at Grinder's Stand, some cabins in the woods of Tennessee. That night two shots were heard from the cabin where Lewis was sleeping. Mrs. Grinder was scared because her husband was away. Lewis staggered out of his cabin and begged for water and first aid, but she kept the door closed all night. Lewis died the next morning and was buried beside the road. Historians still debate whether he committed suicide or whether he was killed by robbers. The man who found his body believed he had been shot in the back. There were no powder burns on his clothes or skin, as there should have been if he had shot himself. His money was missing, and his trunks of papers had been gone through. Suicide was also a possibility. He was behaving strangely, apparently was drunk, and had already tried to take his life twice on this trip. Jefferson believed it was suicide. Clark thought it was suicide at first, but in later years he changed his mind. At age 35, Meriwether Lewis, one of America's greatest explorers, was gone.

Lewis and Clark Portraits Activity

Make your own silhouette.

The following are portraits of Meriwether Lewis and William Clark:

Meriwether Lewis (1774-1809)
Lewis liked to dress in the latest fashion and had the good manners of a Virginia gentleman.

William Clark (1770-1838)
Clark was over six feet (1.82 m) tall and had very red hair.

Silhouettes of famous people are often used as decorations, such as this silhouette of Lewis by Dolley Madison.

Make a silhouette of a friend or have someone make one of you.

1. Have your friend sit in a chair next to a wall, with his or her side toward the wall.
2. Tape paper to the wall at the level of the friend's head. Silhouettes are often done on black paper, but that is your choice.
3. Set up a light source and shine it straight at the paper, past the friend's head, so that a shadow is cast on the paper. This can be from a gooseneck lamp or slide projector. If this is in a classroom, the friend can stand and the light can come from an overhead projector.
4. Remind the person to sit very still. Trace around the shadow of the profile. If you have used black paper, do the tracing with chalk.
5. Carefully remove the paper from the wall. The silhouette can be cut out or it can be left on the paper and colored.

Lewis Prepared for the Expedition

Washington, D.C., to Wood River, Illinois
Mid-March–December 12, 1803

By 1802 it was clear that President Jefferson was already preparing Lewis to head a westward expedition. Jefferson told a friend that what he wanted for an expedition leader was a person "perfectly skilled in botany, natural history, mineralogy, astronomy, with at the same time the necessary firmness of body & mind, habits of living in the woods & familiarity with the Indian character." He knew Lewis was already skilled in frontier living and Indian relations but could learn the sciences. Lewis often went to the President's home at Monticello to use his magnificent personal library. Jefferson also sent Lewis to study with some of the country's leading scientists. This was the first government-sponsored scientific trip for the United States. It was important for Lewis to be well trained.

Lewis left Washington, D.C., in March 1803, first for the federal armory at Harpers Ferry, Virginia (now West Virginia). He purchased rifles, pistols, pipe tomahawks, and knives. The fifteen rifles he ordered were the brand-new Harpers Ferry Model 1803, short-barreled, .54-caliber flintlocks that had just been adopted as the army's official rifle. (.44-caliber Kentucky long rifles were added later.) He ordered 176 pounds (79 kg) of the best gunpowder to be packed in waterproof lead canisters. Lewis also watched the construction of a portable iron-frame boat he designed. He bought clothing, blankets, knapsacks, and tools.

Lewis continued on to Lancaster, Pennsylvania, to visit astronomer Andrew Ellicott. Ellicott spent seventeen long days teaching Lewis the skill of using instruments to determine latitude and longitude. Lewis spent May in Philadelphia where he bought maps and learned more about surveying, plant and animal classifications, and fossils.

In Philadelphia he bought surveying and navigation equipment. As an experienced soldier, Lewis knew what camp equipment was needed, so he bought tents, tools, and cooking utensils. He bought material to make mosquito netting and an air gun. The air gun was not very practical because it had little power or accuracy, but when the Indians saw it could shoot without a loud noise or any smoke, they were very impressed. He also added four tin horns, to be sounded in order to call the soldiers together. He purchased 193 pounds (87 kg) of "portable soup." This was beef boiled down to a thick liquid, with egg whites and chopped vegetables added. After more boiling it became a thick paste. Then this stiff goo was sealed into lead canisters. After the soup was diluted and eaten, the containers could be melted down and molded into bullets. Lewis also bought twenty barrels of flour, and seven barrels each of salt, tea, and cornmeal. Food was less of a priority than many other items because it was expected they would live off the land by hunting and fishing.

Benjamin Rush, the country's most noted physician, recommended medical supplies and gave advice on health care. Lewis bought $94.49 worth of medical supplies from Dr. Rush. In those days, no one knew of bacteria or viruses. A sick body was cured by draining away whatever had invaded it. He bought six hundred of the doctor's famous bilious pills, a powerful and fast-acting laxative known humorously as "Rush's Thunderbolts." Most of the medicines were to cause vomiting, sweating, increased salivation, and kidney output. He also bought pulverized Peruvian bark which contained quinine for treating malaria and strong wine to be used as medicine. Lewis also expected to make use of natural medicines gathered along the route from plants. A few basic surgical instruments were also included.

Finally, Lewis bought $2000 worth of items under the general heading of "Indian presents." Giving gifts to Indians was a time-honored tradition, one that the Indians had come to expect. All peace councils would include gift giving. The most impressive of the gifts were the Indian peace medals. Other presents included brightly colored ribbons, scarlet cloth, glass and pewter beads, fishhooks, knives, needles, bells, paints, rings, flags, calico shirts, small mirrors, combs, tobacco, and more. When the expedition's food ran low or game was difficult to find, the group planned on using their trade goods to buy food from the Indians. Before leaving Philadelphia, Lewis made arrangements to have his supplies transported to Pittsburgh, the city on the Ohio River where he would start west by boat. In June he headed back to Washington for final instructions from Jefferson and to choose Clark as his partner.

After leaving Washington on July 5, Lewis went to Pittsburgh to supervise the construction of the keelboat that was designed to carry ten tons (9 tonnes) of cargo yet not float deep in the water. Lewis was slow leaving Pittsburgh due to repeated delays because the workmen were "incorrigible drunkards." It was supposed to be ready July 20 but wasn't finished until August 31. It is not clear where, but a red and a white pirogue were also purchased. These were flat-bottomed, large dugout "canoes." Apparently at Pittsburgh, Lewis also bought Seaman, his Newfoundland dog.

Lewis finally set out in the keelboat at 11:00 on the morning of August 31, 1803. That day he made his first entry in his journal, a small leather-bound notebook. He was slowed by low water. Horses or oxen had to be hired at times to drag the boat across sandbars. He did not arrive in Louisville, where Clark was waiting for him, until about October 15. There, several men signed up to join the expedition. They left Louisville on October 26 and continued down the Ohio, reaching its confluence with the Mississippi on November 20. It was too late in the year to set off up the Missouri, so they decided to wait until spring. Clark traveled upriver looking for the best spot to establish a winter camp. His hunters reported that the countryside was beautiful and had plenty of game such as turkeys, grouse, opossums, rabbits, and deer.

Lewis Prepared for the Expedition Activity

It took Jefferson, Lewis, and Clark many years of hard work to plan and prepare for exploring the Louisiana Purchase and the Pacific Northwest. It was a challenging and dangerous trip, yet exciting and rewarding.

Plan an imaginary expedition of your own. Think about the following things, and then write them in a letter to your friends, inviting them to go on this journey with you. You can write just one letter addressed "Dear Friends." Use correct friendly format when writing your letter.

Your letter needs to include each of the numbered items. (Don't put the numbers in your letter.) The questions that are asked are to help you with your planning, but it is not necessary (and would not make sense) to answer all of them.

1. *Where will you go?* Will it be to a place that is still unexplored, like outer space? Will you go back in time and pretend you are leading an expedition to lands that were unknown then, such as exploring the jungles of the Amazon River in South America? Will you go even further back in time where no people ever went, such as during the Age of Dinosaurs? Will you become miniaturized and explore something small such as inside a human body or inside a flower?
2. *Why did you choose this particular place to explore?* Is it a place you have studied? Is it somewhere in your imagination? Do you know a lot about the place? Is it important to civilization that you learn about it? Are there people who would not want you to go there?
3. *Who will you take along with you?* Will these be friends that you have today, or will you make up imaginary new friends to take along? Will your pets come with you? How about parents and teachers? How big will the group be? Why did you choose these people? Do some of them have special skills that will be helpful to the group?
4. *When will you go?* Will it be at a particular season? Time of day? Period in history? When you are an adult or a child? During a certain type of weather?
5. *What kinds of preparation will you need to make before you go?* Will you do all of the work yourself? What could others do to help you? Will you need special permission for anything you plan to do on the trip? What kind of food will you take? What kind of equipment is important? What kind of medicine and first aid supplies will you need? What kind of transportation will you use? What kind of clothes will be necessary? What will you take for money or for trading? What kind of training do you need so you have all the necessary skills? What do you already know about this place that you can teach the other members of your group? Do you need tents or other shelter?
6. *How will you want to report your findings to the world when you return?* Will you be willing to be on TV and radio talk shows and the news? Will you let newspapers interview and photograph you? Will you write a book about your findings? Will you keep a journal of written descriptions and pictures while on your trip so your reporting will be accurate and detailed?
7. *Other:* Tell anything else you can think of that would help your friends know what kind of expedition is being planned and that will help them make up their minds if they should go with you.

Winter Preparations at Fort Wood

Wood River, Illinois, to St. Charles, Missouri
December 13, 1803–May 21, 1804

On December 13, Clark established their winter camp along the Wood River in today's Illinois. For the next five months Camp Wood (also known as Camp Dubois) would be the winter quarters for the expedition. The men built log huts and a stockade. The winter was cold and wet, but the fort usually kept them dry, warm, and comfortable. On January 9, however, while hiking through the snow to examine a nearby Indian mound, Clark broke through the ice of a slough. When he got back to camp, he found his feet frozen into his shoes, "which rendered precautions necessary to prevent frost bite."

At Camp Wood, the captains selected and disciplined their men. Lewis and Clark gathered their troops from frontiersmen in the Ohio Valley, from army men at nearby military posts, and from French boatmen near St. Louis. Lewis said he was looking for "good hunters, stout, healthy, unmarried men, accustomed to the woods, and capable of bearing bodily fatigue in a pretty considerable degree." They shaped the new recruits into a tough, well-disciplined crew that became known as the "Corps of Discovery." Originally, plans called for a group of only ten or twelve men, but it was decided that a much larger number was needed in order to move the heavy keelboat and pirogues upriver and provide security against Indian attack. The long winter helped them weed out a few undesirables and to enlist soldiers that were not already in the army.

The Corps of Disovery at Camp Dubois apparently totaled about forty men, counting some French hired hands whose number is uncertain. In their minds, Lewis and Clark always separated the men into two groups—those of the permanent party who would travel the full route and those on temporary assignment to the first winter camp. The temporary group would return the unwieldy keelboat to St. Louis and carry messages for Jefferson. By April 1, 1804, the group was complete, although some changes were made during the expedition.

For most of the winter Clark kept command at Camp Wood while Lewis gained information for their trip from fur traders in nearby St. Louis. (In St. Louis he also managed to acquire some of the first matches ever made, splinters of wood first dipped in sulphur and then in phosphorus. It was twenty years before matches were in general use.) Although there is no record of military drilling, the men probably carried out the usual duties of frontier soldiers. Clark was a former army officer used to strict military procedures. That winter they learned the skills they would need on the trip, tested equipment, worked on the boats, hunted, gathered advice from experienced river travelers, and visited with the neighboring Kickapoo, Sauk, and Delaware Indians.

When the ice broke in the river and spring arrived, activity became intense in the camp. They took practice runs in the boats and packed and loaded supplies. Clark's journal entries grew shorter as he became busier. Finally on the morning of departure, May 14, 1804, he simply wrote, "fixing for a Start." That day Lewis was in St. Louis making final arrangements and would ride overland to meet them at St. Charles, a few miles up the river. At four o'clock in the afternoon, amid cheers of local settlers, the men fired the keelboat's swivel gun and set out. They arrived in St. Charles on May 16. There the loads in the boats were rearranged, some last-minute supplies were purchased, extra boatmen were hired, and parties were held in their honor. On Sunday, May 20, the men attended mass. Lewis arrived that evening, and the expedition was ready to begin.

Discipline Among the Corps of Discovery

During the winter at Fort Wood, almost all of the men of the expedition had to be disciplined for their behavior. Most of the discipline was for drunkenness, fighting, leaving without permission, or not obeying orders. Some of it was due to men who were not used to military discipline. In other cases it was probably due to being in close quarters for long periods of time and boredom. Some of the men most often disciplined, such as John Colter and Reuben Field, eventually turned out to be the most able and reliable men of the Corps.

When there was a discipline problem, there was usually a court martial, which was a military trial. The jury was made of other members of the expedition. A common form of discipline was flogging, which was a severe whipping with a strap or stick. Sometimes Clark came up with more creative punishments. For example, when Privates John Potts and William Werner got into a bloody fistfight, he had them work off their excess energy by building a cabin for a local woman who had offered to serve as the camp laundress. On the positive side, he often rewarded good deeds with extra rations of whiskey or winners of shooting contests with small amounts of prize money.

In April both captains had to be gone. The men disobeyed Ordway, who had been left in charge. When Clark returned he found drunken, disrespectful men. To restore order he thought up chores. For example, he had the keelboat turned over on its side, and the men had to patch every crack. As the men began to show they were sorry, Clark ordered target practice which they enjoyed and set up shooting contests with the nearby settlers.

The last court martial Lewis and Clark conducted was for Private John Newman for insubordination. Punishment was seventy-five lashes, dismissal from the Corps, and being demoted to common boatman. The Arikara Indians who witnessed the whipping were appalled. Clark wrote on October 14, "The punishment of this day allarmed. the Indian Chief verry much. he cried aloud. . . I explained the Cause of the punishment and the necessity [of it] which he also thought examples were also necessary, & he himself had made them by Death, [but] his nation never whiped even their Children, from their burth."

Only a few times were court martials needed on the entire journey. This shows the men respected Lewis and Clark. Clark tried to instill pride in the men and told them to behave to show a "true respect for their own dignity."

Winter Preparations at Fort Wood Activity

Imagine you were leading an expedition into an unknown, dangerous area. Describe the kinds of discipline you would have for your group. What would the rules and punishment be? What would you do for the group when they behaved especially well? How would you behave so the group would respect you so much that they would want to behave, even if there weren't rules?

Beginning Days of the Expedition

Along the Lower Missouri River
Past St. Charles, Missouri, to Council Bluffs, Iowa
May 22–August 3, 1804

The trip up the lower Mississippi River was slow and difficult. The water level was high in the spring, and they were traveling against the current. Snags and hidden rocks made it dangerous. The boats ran aground on shifting sandbars, which were almost impossible to see through the muddy water. The easiest traveling came when there was a good breeze for sailing. Otherwise, when the bank was firm, the men jumped ashore and pulled the boats upstream by rope. Sometimes they moved the boats with poles or paddles. Sometimes the bank collapsed into the river, almost crushing the men. When this happened, whole trees were uprooted and flew down the river. On June 28 Clark wrote, “passed a bad Sand bar, where our tow rope broke twice, & with great exertions, we rowed around it and came to & camped.” Men spent hours on end up to their waists in the swift river, and went for days without ever getting completely dry. It was hard work, from sunup to sundown in eighty- to ninety-degree (26 to 32° C) temperatures. Clark wrote that the men sweated more than he thought humanly possible. During this stretch of the river, they made an average progess of nine to ten miles (14.5 to 16 km) per day.

They quickly settled into the routine of life on the river, learning to work as a team. They shared responsibilities so that each man had a turn at many kinds of jobs. Lewis explored along the shore with Seaman. Clark usually stayed with the boats because he was a better riverman. He kept a compass reading for every shift in direction, made accurate guesses of the distances, and calculated the length of each day’s travel. For example, at the mouth of the Platte River he announced they had come six hundred miles (966 km) from the mouth of the Missouri. Instrument measurements made several years later gave a total of 611 miles (983.7 km).

Each day several men hunted for game. They had little problem finding enough wild fruit, fish, vegetables, and game to feed the expedition that first summer. The hunters rode ahead on their horses and when they had killed a deer, bear, elk, or a bison, they hung the carcass on a tree, leaning out over the river. As the boats made their way up the river, the men loaded the meat on board. Clark wrote on June 17, “George Drewyer our hunter came in with 2 Deer & a Bear, also a young Horse been in the Prarie a long time and is fat.” It took good hunting to feed the hungry men. The cooks prepared only one big meal a day, in the evening. There were cold leftovers for breakfast and lunch.

Even during these beginning days, there were plenty of adventures. A little beyond today’s Matson, Missouri, are three hundred-foot (91-meter) white limestone cliffs beside the river. On May 23 Lewis was exploring the land above the cliffs when his foothold crumbled. He slid and bounced downward about twenty feet (6 m) but saved himself by sticking his knife in the rock.

Clark wrote on July 4, “Jos. Fields got bit, by a snake, which was quickly doctored with bark by Cap. Lewis. July 7. one man verry sick. Struck with the Sun.” Mosquitoes, flies, ticks, and chiggers tormented the sweating men. For a repellent they smeared their skin with bear grease. Sore feet, boils, heat stroke, dysentery, and rheumatism were common. However, on July 20 Clark commented that he felt the party had been much healthier than groups in similar situations.

Peace Councils with the Indian Tribes

Whenever they could, Lewis and Clark held peace councils with the Indian tribes in an effort to win their loyalty to the United States. In order for the expedition to be an economic and political success, it was important to win the respect and friendship of the Indian tribes they met. When the expedition met with a chief of a large tribe, there was often a ceremony lasting several hours. During this ceremony, Lewis and Clark would try to impress upon the chief the importance of making and keeping peace. If the chief would promise to be under the rule of the "Great Chief" (President Jefferson), and if he would make peace with all of the other tribes in the area, then they would give him a peace medal as a symbol of their agreement.

Peace medals began with George Washington and continued into the 1880s. The first ones were made by hand and later by the U.S. Mint. All medals roughly followed a similar style. The image of the current President was on the face of the medal with his name and date of inauguration. The reverse side displayed two hands clasped in friendship and a tomahawk crossed by a peace pipe. Usually the handshake showed one military cuff and one bare wrist. The Jefferson medal varies in that the Indian wrist is adorned with a fancy bracelet, perhaps to indicate a very important chief. Five sizes of medals were taken on the expedition, for chiefs of varying importance.

The first of many councils with Indian tribes took place north of today's Omaha, Nebraska, at a place the captains called "Councile Bluff." The council was held on August 3, 1804, with six Oto and Missouri chiefs. (So many of the Missouri Indians had died from disease that they had joined with the Otos for safety. Sadly, the Indians had no resistance to European diseases that they had gotten from the fur traders. Smallpox was the worst, wiping out entire villages at a time, but even measles was deadly to these people.) Since this was their first Indian council, the expedition spent the night with "every man on his Guard & ready for any thing," as Clark noted. Lewis and Clark didn't know what to expect, but they treated the Indians with dignity. President Jefferson's instructions to Lewis had made it clear that he wanted them to act as ambassadors. They met under an awning of sailcloth. The ceremony included a parade, speeches by one of the captains and the chief, smoking the peace pipe, awarding peace medals and certificates to the Indians, and exchanging gifts. There was also an exchange of food. The Indians gave watermelons and were given roast meat and flour. To awe the natives, Lewis and Clark showed off their technology. They demonstrated the use of the air gun, magnet, spyglass, compass, and watch. The air gun caused a sensation among the Indians, who thought it was magic. Although it was difficult to communicate, the Indians were informed that the land had passed from Spain to France to the United States. This must have sounded odd to the Indians because they had no concept of land ownership.

Beginning Days of the Expedition Activity

Imagine that you have been asked to bring peace between yourself and a fictitious group you might meet on the expedition you designed in the first activity.

Do the following:

1. Design and draw both sides of a peace medal that you can give these people.
2. Write a description of the meaning of your peace medal. For example, with the Jefferson medal, the crossed tomahawk and peace pipe meant "peace over war."
3. Write a description of all the parts of your peace ceremony, in the order in which you would do them. For example, in the peace council with the Otos and Missouris, one of the things Lewis did was shoot off the air gun to show his power.

The Northern Great Plains of the Missouri River

Between Council Bluffs, Iowa, and Washburn, North Dakota
August 4–October 25, 1804

The only death of the expedition occurred on August 20 near Sioux City, Iowa, where Sergeant Charles Floyd died. He had been in great pain and could not keep food down. As he died he whispered to Clark, "I'm going away." His friends buried him on a nearby hill. It is thought that Floyd had a ruptured appendix which, in 1804, could not have been treated anywhere.

The Yankton Sioux warmly greeted Lewis and Clark. Clark wrote about their tipis on August 29, "the Scioues Camps are handsom of a Conic form Covered with Buffalow Roabs Painted different colours." The next day he described the people, "The Souex is a Stout bold lookin people.. make use of Bows & arows the Wariers are Verry much deckerated with Paint Porcupine quils & feathers, large legins and mockersons, all with buffalow roabs of Different Colours." A few days before, the expedition had an unusual experience. Some of the men marched a long distance to see what the Indians called "the Mountain of the Little People." The Indians claimed that the little devils were savage fighters in human form, just eighteen inches (46 cm) tall. Only the bravest warriors would go near this mountain with Lewis and Clark, but they had found nothing.

In September, seventeen-year-old George Shannon became lost. He had been hunting and had stopped to rest. When he awoke he thought the boats had passed him. For two weeks he tried to catch up with the boats. By whittling substitute bullets out of wood he had managed to kill a rabbit, but when that was gone he had only grapes and wild plums to eat. Finally, he started walking downstream hoping that a fur trader would float by but was very surprised when he saw the keelboat coming *upstream*. The boats had not passed him after all!

One of their most dramatic times started on September 23 when the expedition met the Teton Sioux near today's Pierre, South Dakota. Lewis and Clark had been warned that these Sioux had all but closed the Missouri River to white traders trying to go upstream by demanding huge tolls and robbing the boats. They were also raiding the villages of other Indian tribes. For several days things were tense with uncomfortable peace councils and standoffs with weapons. Since the Tetons wanted *all* of the expedition's supplies and trade goods, giving in to their demands was impossible. The Indians finally backed down when Clark aimed the boat's large swivel gun into the crowd of warriors. The Tetons were greatly impressed by this bravery, and word of this courage spread up and down the river.

On October 8, the expedition came to the villages of the friendly Arikara Indians. They were farmers rather than hunters and lived year-round in earthen lodges. Clark wrote, "Those people are Durtey, Kind, pore, & extravigent. [They] gave us to eate bread made of Corn & Beens, also Corn & Beans boild. a large Been which is rich & verry nurrishing also Squashes &c. all Tranquillity." They had a peace council and traded goods, but they were most interested in Clark's slave, York, and examined him with much curiosity. Clark wrote on October 9, "[Indians] much astonished at my black Servent, who did not lose the opportunity of [displaying] his powers of Strength &c. &c. this nation never Saw a black man before." York was very strong and intelligent. He roared at the Indian children who screamed delightedly. York was a good actor and told the Indians how he had been a wild animal "and lived upon people" until caught and tamed by Clark. Clark felt he somewhat overdid it, "he Carried on the joke and made himself more turribal than we wished him to doe." Some Indians believed that York's black skin was paint and some of the women boldly tried to rub it off.

Nature Journals

President Jefferson had discovered the fossil of a giant ground sloth (named Megalonyx jefferson) which he proudly displayed in the East Room of the White House. The President wondered if this animal might still exist in the unexplored West. Lewis and Clark didn't find the giant sloth but did record information in their journals about the pronghorn, badger, coyote, white-tailed jack rabbit, fossils, western grey fox, a new kind of deer which they called the "mule deer" because of its large ears, and more. While they waited at Fort Mandan, Lewis and Clark also prepared artifacts to be sent to Jefferson with some men who were returning from the trip in the spring. These included plant and animal specimens that were new to science. They sent back cages containing a live prairie dog, a sharp-tailed grouse, and four magpies. They sent the horns of a bighorn sheep, skins and skeletons of antelopes, jack rabbits, badgers, a coyote, and a grizzly bear. Samples of earth, salt, and minerals were in the shipment. Most of the artifacts reached Washington, D.C. Not many explorers in the history of the world have provided such detailed and accurate information on the regions they explored. Here are some of the things they described.

When the hunters returned to camp each day, Lewis always asked them for descriptions of the soil and vegetation they had seen. Clark noted, "I walked out three miles, found the prarie composed of good Land. . . with points of timber land. Those Praries are not like those, E. Of the Mississip-pi, void of every thing except grass, they abound with Hasel Grapes & wild plumb. . . ."

They enjoyed watching birds too. Clark wrote, "Great numbers of Birds are seen Such as black bird, ren, or Prarie bird, a kind of larke about the size of a Partridge." Lewis was intrigued with the magpie, ". . . wings to center of the back is White, the Beeke like a Crow, abt the Size of a large Pigeon. a butifull thing."

Clark described the first prairie dog village they saw, "discovered a Village of Small animals that burrow in the grown. . . Cought one a live by poreing a great quantity of Water in his hole. . . great numbers of holes on the top of which those little animals Set erect make Whistleing noise and whin allarmed. . . ."

Lewis described beaver, "there were three beaver taken this morning the men prefer the flesh of this anamal, to that of any other which we have, I eat very heartily of the beaver myself, and think it excellent; particularly the tale, and liver."

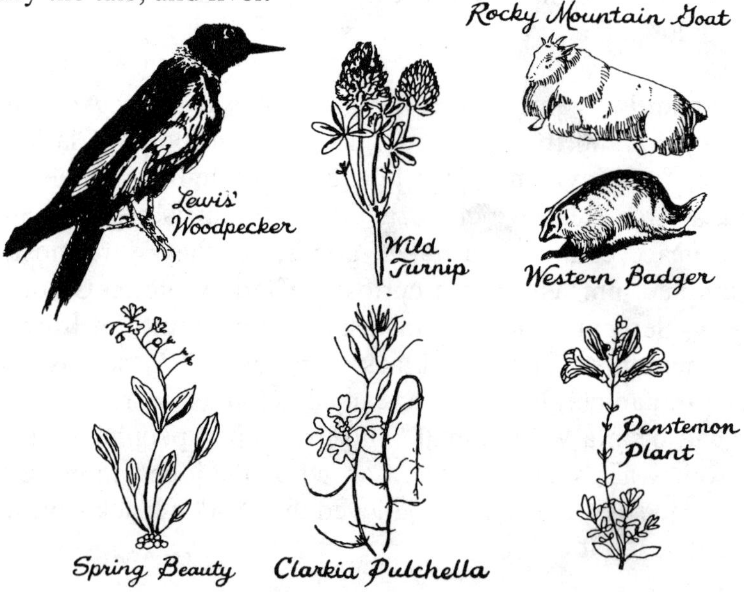

The Northern Great Plains of the Missouri River Activity

During the winter of 1804-05, Lewis and Clark used part of their time at Fort Mandan to catch up with their journal writing, to add details, and to be sure their records of the plants, animals, and geology were accurate. Their journals were written in twenty small notebooks. As each was filled, it was put into a small tin box and sealed to keep it waterproof. Thanks to these precautions, all their journals survived the trip. You can be a nature journalist too.

Bind a book and make a nature journal.

1. Put at least ten pages in your book.
2. Page 1 should be a title page. Tell the title of the book, your name, the date, and put a colored picture of nature on this page.
3. On pages 2 to 10, draw detailed pictures and write complete descriptions of each item. Be sure you have some plants, some animals, *and* some geology.
4. When you write this nature journal, pretend you are Lewis or Clark, and you must work so accurately that someone who has never seen what you are drawing will know all about it by what you say and draw.

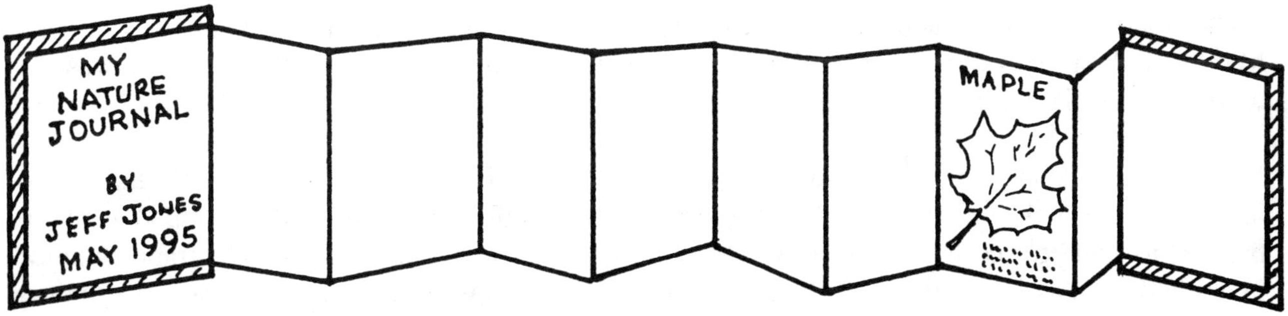

Winter at Fort Mandan

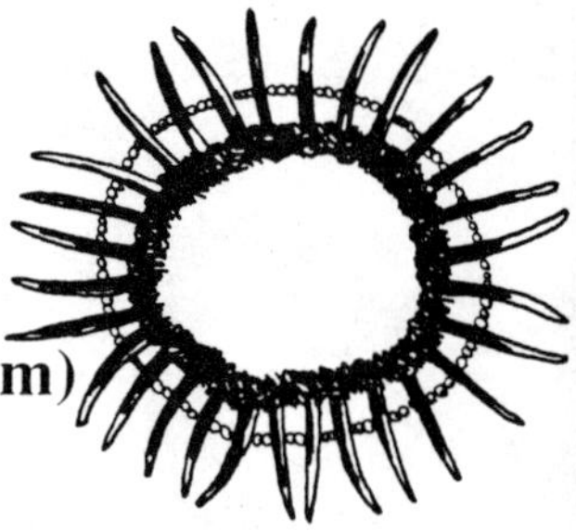

Confluence of Missouri and Knife Rivers
Near Washburn, North Dakota, About 60 Miles (96.6 km) Upstream from Bismarck
October 26, 1804–April 7, 1805

Lewis and Clark were anxious to reach the Mandan villages and get their winter quarters built. The Missouri River would soon freeze, ending their travel until spring. They finally arrived on October 26 and had a council with the Indians. Since Lewis and Clark knew about the Mandans, they probably decided before leaving St. Louis that they would try to spend the winter here. Maps of that time would have shown the Mandan villages because, unlike most other plains tribes, these Indians weren't nomadic and trappers had visited them for years. Of the five Indian villages, two were Mandan, two were Hidatsas, and one was Ahaharways, related to the Hidatsas. The tribes had been weakened by smallpox and by the warring Sioux. They were now living near one another for protection. These tribes lived in earthen lodges and had a history of being friendly to the whites. Clark said, "These are the most friendly, well disposed Indians inhabiting the missouri. They are brave, humane, and hospitable."

They selected a site for their fort a few miles downstream from the Mandan villages. By November 3 they started to build the fort and by November 20 they were able to move in. They finished just in time because by November 28, the river was choked with ice and it began to snow. It turned out to be a very cold winter. Clark recorded temperatures down to 45 degrees below zero (-43° C). One fur trader tried to write a letter and said, "The ink freezes in my pen, though I sit so close to the fire as I can without burning my leg." The fort was built of cottonwood and consisted of a lookout tower and two rows of connected cabins. It was built so well that one trader said it was "so strong as to be almost cannonball proof." Lewis wrote, "This place we have named Fort Mandan in honour of our Neighbours." The fort flew the American flag and, at that time, was the westernmost military outpost of the United States.

Lewis and Clark spent more than five busy months at Fort Mandan. The captains used the time to learn as much as they could about the Missouri River ahead. French and British trappers came to the fort to trade for corn. Lewis and Clark could learn about the land from these trappers since many had been as far upstream as the confluence of the Yellowstone River. There was also much to learn from the Indians, especially the Hidatsas, who traveled as far west as the Rocky Mountains to raid other tribes. They learned about mountain passes, waterfalls, rivers, and other landmarks they would pass in their travels. In addition to learning about possible routes, equipment was inspected and repaired and there was plenty of firewood to cut. They made hides into new clothing. Clark drew maps of their journey. Lewis completed his nature collection to send east in the spring to President Jefferson. Medical treatment was given to the Indians, such as the time it was so cold that Lewis had to amputate the frozen toes of a boy. They also studied Indian cultures. Clark watched a three-day bison dance, but they misunderstood some activities and also missed some important ceremonies because they stayed only part of the year. However, during their stay at Fort Mandan the captains did some of their best Indian studies. They also seemed to find ways to amuse themselves. Peter Cruzatte played his fiddle, and they danced many nights. It's rather amazing, but somehow Cruzatte kept the fiddle from getting smashed, warped, or stolen throughout the whole journey.

John Shields built a small forge and made iron weapons and tools. The hatchets he made from a damaged stove became prized possessions of the chiefs. Some of his tools were traded to the Indians for food. They brought corn, pemmican, jerked meat, dried pumpkins, squashes, and beans. Pemmican is a food unique to North American Indians. It was made from lean bison meat or venison cut in thin slices, dried in the sun, pounded fine, mixed with melted fat and sometimes berries, and packed in sacks of hide. For a while, meat was plentiful, but as the winter wore on, the hunters had to travel farther to find anything to shoot. Sheheke, a Mandan chief, taught Clark how to kill bison with a bow and arrow so that the expedition's ammunition supply could be saved. It is estimated that it took one bison or four deer to feed the group each day.

For over a month, they struggled to free their boats from the three-foot (91-centimeter)-thick ice in the river. Lewis wrote on February 3, "the situation of our boat and perogues is now allarming, they are firmly inclosed in the Ice and almost covered with snow. . . ." They had to chop their pirogues out of the ice and haul them to the fort for repairs. The navigable part of the river would be narrower from here on, and the keelboat was now too big. A group went upstream and found cottonwood trees big enough to make six dugout canoes which they covered with pitch for waterproofing. One day the ice broke in the river, and the men saw an astonishing sight. Bloated carcasses of bison that had drowned during the winter were floating downstream. They were being caught by the Indians who leaped from ice floe to ice floe to get lines around them. There were great feasts of "ripe" bison meat. One man's journal described this, "the flesh is a greenish hue. . . and so ripe, so tender, that very little boiling is necessary–the stench is intolerable–yet the soup they make from it. . . is reckoned delicious."

When the Missouri River was free of ice, they were able to continue on their expedition. On April 7, some of the men started back to St. Louis in the keelboat. Those leaving were Corporal Warfington and a small squad of soldiers, the remaining French boatmen, and the two expelled men, Reed and Newman. They took nine boxes containing the nature collection, detailed maps, Indian artifacts, journals, letters to families and friends, and letters to President Jefferson. (The keelboat got back to St. Louis on May 20, and the precious cargo eventually arrived in Washington, D.C., to President Jefferson's complete delight and fascination.) On that day Lewis wrote, "Having on this day at 4 P.M. completed every arrangement necessary for our departure, we dismissed the barge and crew with orders to return without loss of time to St. Louis. at the same moment that the Barge departed from Fort Mandan, Capt. Clark embarked with our party and proceeded up the River. as I had used no exercise for several weeks, I determined to walk on shore."

Celebrating Holidays

Journals of the Lewis and Clark expedition describe some holidays during the trip such as Christmas, New Year's Day, birthdays, and the Fourth of July.

While they were at Fort Mandan, they celebrated Christmas. The men woke up their captains with rifle shots and a salute. Clark responded by giving them some rum to drink. Rum was given out only on days that had been especially hard or when some difficult task had been accomplished. This was Christmas, though, and they wanted to celebrate. They drank a toast to the health of President Jefferson, and John Colter raised the American flag. The Indians had been told to stay away from the fort on this day because it was a "great medicine day," meaning an important ceremony. Peter Cruzatte played his fiddle and one room was cleared for dancing. They feasted on bread baked from a limited supply of flour, pies made of dried apples, and pepper-spiced steaks. After a while some of the men became bored and went hunting.

Sergeant Ordway explained in his journal, "We fired the Swivels [cannons] at day break & each man fired one round. our officers Gave the party a drink of Taffe [rum]. we had the Best to eat that could be had, & continued firing dancing & frolicking dureing the whole day. the [Indians] did not Trouble us as we had requested them not to come as it was a great medician day with us. We enjoyed a merry christmas dureing the day & evening untill nine oClock–all in peace and quietness."

On New Year's Day Lewis and Clark permitted sixteen of the men to visit the nearest Mandan village in the morning, carrying with them "a fiddle & a Tambereen & a Sounden horn [bugle]." They fired a rifle salute outside the village and were invited in. The Indians were excited by their dancing. One of the Frenchmen did a jig while standing on his hands. On January 2, the other half of the men who had not celebrated the day before got their turn in the Mandan village.

Shortly after New Year's, one village of Mandans held a celebration of their own. The whites referred to it as the Buffalo Calling Dance. To the Indians it was the Red Stick Ceremony. The purpose of this ceremony was to call back the bison that had wandered far away, leaving the Indians short of food. Four days after the ceremony, the bison did return, along with elk.

Winter at Fort Mandan Activity I

Imagine you were a person your age going on the Lewis and Clark expedition. Choose a holiday and describe how you would have celebrated it.

Do the following:

1. Tell the name of the holiday and write a description of how you would celebrate this special day. It can be a new holiday that did not exist then, but you can use only the supplies the Lewis and Clark expedition took with them. For example, you could not have a CD player!
2. They obviously did not have invitations on the expedition, but just for fun, design an invitation to this holiday celebration. Color the front of the invitation. On the inside be sure to tell the five W's of the event: who, what, where, when, why.

Types of Indian Houses and Shelters

Clark described the houses of the Mandans, Hidatsas, and Ahaharways, the Indians around whom they spent the winter of 1804-05, "[They] Live in warm houses, large and built in an [octagonal] form forming a cone at top which is left open for the smoke to pass, those houses are Generally 30 or 40 foot Diamiter, Covd. with earth on poles willows & grass to prevent the earths passing thro."

The houses were solidly constructed and lasted about ten years. This part of today's North Dakota has little rainfall, about 16" (41 cm) a year. These log and earth-covered houses could not have stood heavy rains. The villages were surrounded by ditches and embankments for protection against the Sioux. Lewis and Clark reported that in cold weather, the Indians brought their best horses and dogs inside the houses at night. These Indians lived in fairly permanent villages. They were not nomadic. Instead of traveling to find their food, they were mostly farmers who grew corn, beans, and squash and gathered some native plants. Today, visitors can see remnants of this type of house at the Knife River Indian Villages National Historic Site and North Dakota's Fort Lincoln State Park. These tribes used only the skin tipi several times a year on bison-hunting trips.

Winter at Fort Mandan Activity II

Research the types of homes that other Indians had. These should be Indians that Lewis and Clark met on their travels. You can build models, draw pictures, and/or write detailed descriptions.

The tribes listed below are some of the tribes Lewis and Clark met. When you look for these names in books, be aware that they are often spelled in different ways or even have different names for the same tribes. Research one or more of them. As you read about the Indians, learn why they would build houses the way they did. For example, a tribe that was nomadic would have found the tipi to be very convenient because it would have been easy to move.

Ahahami, Ahaharway, Wattersoons, or Wattason
Arikara, Arickaree, Recare, or Ree
Blackfoot
Chinook
Clatsop
Flathead, Tushepaw, or Tushepah
Hidatsas, Minitari, Minnetaree, or Gros Ventres
Mandan
Missouri
Nez Perce or Chopunnish
Oto
Shoshone, Shoshoni, or Snake
Teton Sioux
Tillamook, Callamox, or Killamux
Wahclellah
Walla Walla
Wasco
Wishram
Yakima or Sokulk
Yankton Sioux

Sacagawea, Charbonneau, and Pomp

Sacagawea was born in the 1780s to the Shoshone (Snake) tribe of today's Eastern Idaho in the Rocky Mountains. The Shoshones were nomadic and followed the seasonal plants and game. Her tribe was looking for food when she was captured by the Hidatsas (Minitaris). This was near Three Forks in today's Montana. It is not known how old she was at the time of her capture, but accounts vary from ages nine to fourteen. She was made a slave, moved hundreds of miles away and renamed Tsa-ka-ka-wias, meaning "bird woman." The spelling of her name can be found in different ways. For example, in South Dakota her name is spelled with a *j*–Sacajawea, but North Dakota uses a *k*–Sakakawea. Historians feel the name should be pronounced "Sa-COG-ah-we-ah," so the spelling would be closer to *Sacagawea*. Her husband called her Jenny, but because of his French-Canadian accent, it sounded like "Janey" so that is the nickname the other members of the expedition called her.

Each year, fur trappers, traders, and Indians held a gathering called a rendezvous to trade, gamble, and celebrate. The Hidatsas took Sacagawea to a rendezvous and traded her to the Mandans. She later married Toussaint Charbonneau, a fur trapper and interpreter who was about forty-three years old. He either bought her or won her in a gambling game. Charbonneau was half Sioux and half French Canadian. He had three Indian wives and liked the other two better because they obeyed him. When Sacagawea disobeyed, he sometimes beat her with a stick.

On February 11 when the temperature was 42 degrees below zero (-41° C), Sacagawea gave birth to a baby boy. She was about sixteen years old. Charbonneau named the baby Jean Baptiste, but the expedition called him Pomp, the Shoshone word for "chief" or "firstborn." Her labor was speeded up using a local tradition of swallowing a small part of the rattle of a rattlesnake mixed in water. Pomp was just two months old when they left on the expedition. He rode on Sacagawea's back in a cradleboard. Although it was a difficult journey, Sacagawea worked hard to keep her baby clean. His diapers were often made of moss or cattail fluff in a softly tanned animal skin that could be washed.

During the winter at Fort Mandan, Charbonneau asked to be hired as an interpreter for Lewis and Clark. He had been living with the Hidatsas for about five years and spoke some Indian languages and French, but no English. Some other men would be able to translate the French to English. They were interested in hiring Charbonneau, but they considered him a lazy rascal. Lewis and Clark had learned that they would not be able to cross the Rocky Mountains without horses. Since Sacagawea, Charbonneau's wife, spoke Shoshone, she might be able to get horses from her people. She would also know something about the land they would have to cross. Sacagawea did prove to be very helpful on the trip, but Charbonneau was a constant complainer and not very useful. He probably kept his job because they liked Sacagawea and described her as being gentle and modest.

After the expedition, Sacagawea, Charbonneau, and Pomp returned to the Hidatsa country. Charbonneau was paid wages of $500.33, but Sacagawea received no money. Not much is known of her life after this time. Clark cared very much for Pomp and offered to raise him and give him the finest education. Sacagawea kept Pomp at the end of the expedition but later sent him to be with Clark. Pomp spent five years in Europe where he got a fine education provided by a German prince. He learned several languages. Later he served as an interpreter for the U.S. Army. He became a guide, hunter, and explorer in the West. In 1866, at the age of 61, he left his home in

Auburn, California, where he had been mining for gold, and headed for the gold fields of Montana. On the way, he died of pneumonia and was buried at Inskip Station, near Jordan Valley, Oregon.

Some say Sacagawea left her abusive husband, wandered all over the West, and finally ended up on the Wind River Indian Reservation with other Shoshones. It is said that she served an important role as translator for Chief Washakie in helping establish the reservation. They say she died on April 9, 1884, and is buried at Fort Washakie. This information is based on the testimony of Dr. Charles Eastman. He was a Sioux Indian who investigated the life and death of Sacagawea at the request of the Commissioner of Indian Affairs in 1924. However, others say she died in South Dakota and is buried near Fort Manuel. John Luttig, a fur trapper, wrote in his journal on December 20, 1812, "This Evening the Wife of Charbonneau a Snake Squaw, died of a putrid fever she was a good and the best Women in the fort, aged abt 25 years she life a fine infant girl." Some people feel this was actually one of Charbonneau's other wives. Supporting the South Dakota death theory is a notebook of Clark's. Next to Sacagawea's name is the word *dead.*

Sacagawea was truly a help to Lewis and Clark and has become well known to Americans. There are more statues to honor her than any other American woman. She *did* help the expedition, but mostly not in the role of a guide. Sacagawea was familiar with only a small part of the area through which they traveled and had not been there since she was a child. This myth of being the main guide started when Eva Emery Dye wrote a historical novel called *The Conquest: The True Story of Lewis and Clark,* in 1902, in which she deliberately made Sacagawea "bigger than life" to further the cause of women's rights.

However, Sacagawea helped by knowing about edible roots and berries which were a welcome addition to the meat brought in by the hunters. She showed calm in emergencies and was a good observer. Her presence told the other Indians they met that the expedition was peaceful. War parties never took women or children with them. This may be the main reason the expedition was able to avoid conflicts and to develop good relationships with the tribes they met. She helped interpret among the Shoshone and got horses for the expedition. Clark said this about her help, "She was particularly useful among the Shoshonis. Indeed she has borne with a patience truly admirable the fatigue of so long a route, encumbered with the charge of an infant who is now only 19 months old." She showed strength and courage throughout the trip and had earned the men's respect.

Sacagawea, Charbonneau, and Pomp Activity

Imagine what Sacagawea would have told the Hidatsa Indians when she returned from the journey. Write a description of what Sacagawea told these Indians about:

1. Where she went and what she saw.
2. Her role on the trip (what she contributed to the success of the expedition).

Spring Along the Missouri River

Between Fort Mandan, North Dakota, and the Marias River, Montana
April 7–June 2, 1805

At 4 p.m. on April 7, the same day the keelboat started back to St. Louis, the expedition continued on up the Missouri River with six small dugout canoes and two larger pirogues. There were now thirty-three people which became known as the "permanent party."

It was feeling like spring. The geese were flying north, flowers were blooming on the prairie, and Clark wrote, "the Musquetors troublesom." On April 10 Lewis wrote, "The country on both sides of the missouri. . . is one continued level fertile plain as far as the eye can reach, in which there is not even a solitary tree or shrub to be seen." Clark wrote on April 22, ". . . I had a most delightfull view of the country. . . immence herds of Buffaloe, Elk, deer, & Antelopes feeding in one common and boundless pasture." On April 26 they arrived at the confluence of the Missouri and Yellowstone Rivers. This was a major landmark. Lewis wrote, "all in good health, and much pleased at having arrived at this long wished for spot."

Twice, Charbonneau's clumsiness nearly capsized a pirogue. He didn't get the boat back under control until Cruzatte threatened to shoot him if he didn't "do his duty." Water almost completely filled the boat. They were worried about losing people, valuable papers, medicine, and trade goods for the Indians. It took two days to dry everything out. Sacagawea got the credit for saving most of the things that washed overboard.

Interesting things kept happening. A lone bison charged through their camp in the middle of the night and nearly trampled everyone. Seaman saved the day by his furious barking. Then all in one day, Lewis was charged by a grizzly, a wolverine, and three bison! He was also nearly bitten by a huge rattlesnake. "It. . . seemed to me that all the beasts of the neighborhood had made a league to destroy me, " he wrote. A sandstorm was so thick it looked like smoke. Lewis wrote, ". . . so penitrating is this sand that we. . . are compelled to eat, drink, and breath it very freely." They marveled at bison calves, wolves, bighorn sheep, cliffs of coal, and bird calls. The men gained a healthy respect for grizzly bears after being chased by bears that hadn't been killed, even after being repeatedly shot. The most effective way for the Indians to kill bison was to stampede them over a cliff, but the men were disgusted at the wasted carcasses.

On May 26 Lewis climbed a steep hill and "beheld the Rocky Mountains for the first time. . . were covered with snow and the sun shone on it in such manner as to give me the most plain and satisfactory view." Actually, he was mistaken and really was looking at the Bear's Paw Mountains. Whether he had thought about it before or not, at least now he knew that there would be no easy portage to the Columbia River, that there was no "Northwest Passage." There were still many difficult miles to go. Even though it was spring, at these high mountain elevations it was very cold. They often had to wade in icy water up to their armpits for long periods of time to tow the boats. The mud was so sticky they could not wear moccasins. Their unprotected feet were cut and bruised as they walked over sharp rocks on the river bottom.

Missouri Breaks–White Cliffs

On May 31, 1805, the men spent much of the day in the icy water towing the boats along. There were strong winds full of powdery sand. Clark wrote, "my feet is very much brused & cut walking over the flint, & constantly stuck full of Prickley pear [cactus] thorns, I puled out 17 by the light of the fire to night Musqutors verry troublesom."

The good thing was that they had entered a wildly beautiful stretch of the river known today as the Breaks of the Missouri. On the western end of the Breaks lie the spectacular White Cliffs. Water erosion had worn the white sandstone into amazing shapes. As Lewis wrote on May 31, "The hills and river Clifts which we passed today exhibit a most romantic appearence. The water in the course of time has trickled down the soft sand clifts and woarn it into a thousand grotesque figures, which with the help of a little immagination. . . represent eligant ranges of lofty freestone buildings, having their parapets well stocked with statuary; . . . As we passed on it seemed as if those seens of visionary inchantment would never have an end. . . ." This enchanting section of the river known as the White Cliffs was one of the most memorable natural sights the expedition saw on its trip.

(Note: In this beautiful area lived a large number of Rocky Mountain bighorn sheep. The animals skipped gracefully over rocky hillsides that looked too steep for any hoofed animal to cross. Lewis described them in detail. Unfortunately, this subspecies of the bighorn which Lewis described became the target of hunters and is now extinct.)

Spring Along the Missouri River Activity

Using a dough recipe that can be sculptured, create an imaginary and amazing geological scene such as White Cliffs.

Do the following:

1. Build the scene in a shoe box so it's like you're looking down on it from an airplane. Before you start, cut a window in one end of the box so the viewers will also be able to see the scene as if they were down among the giant rocks taking a hike.
2. Give your scene a name.
3. Write a detailed description of your scene, as if you were Lewis or Clark seeing it for the first time. Write so much detail that President Jefferson would be able to imagine it without ever having seen it. You might want to trade descriptions with your friends and see if you can identify one another's scenes just by what is written.
4. For other ideas you might want to research geological wonders such as Grand Canyon, Bryce, Zion, Yosemite, Monument Valley, craters of the moon.

Here is one recipe you can use.

1 cup (240 ml) cornstarch	$1^1/_4$ cups (300 ml) cold water
2 cups (480 ml) baking soda	food coloring (optional)

Add food coloring to water and mix well with other ingredients in a saucepan. Cook over medium heat about three to four minutes, stirring constantly until the mixture thickens to a consistency of mashed potatoes. Cover with a damp cloth to cool. Knead until smooth. Objects may be left to dry overnight and then painted. Store unused clay in an airtight container.

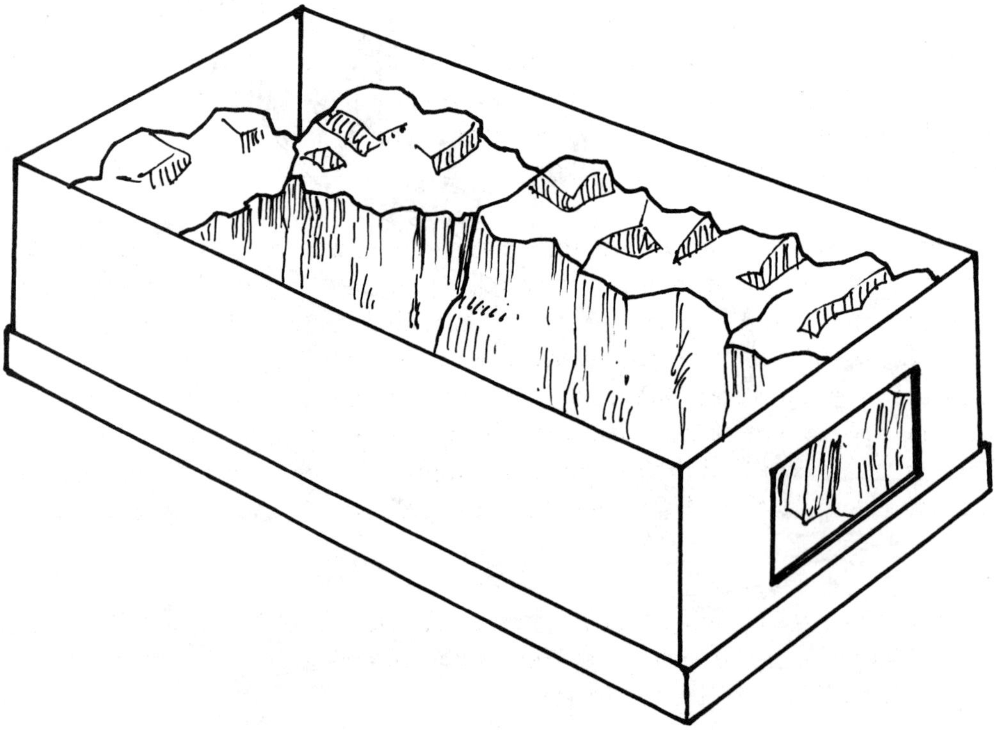

Great Falls of the Missouri

Marias River and Great Falls, Montana
June 3–July 14, 1805

On June 3, Lewis and Clark reached a point where the river seemed to divide into two rivers the same size. They didn't know which branch was the Missouri, the river that would lead to the waterfalls the Hidatsas had told them about. For nine days they explored both branches of the river, the Missouri and the Marias (mar-EYE-as). Although they still were a little confused, they finally decided on the correct branch, the real Missouri River.

Lewis then took four of the men and went on ahead. That day he became very ill with dysentery but cured himself by drinking a mixture of boiled chokecherry twigs that was black and bitter. Clark helped hide one of the pirogues that they now felt they didn't need. It was tied tightly to trees on an island in the Marias River so it would not be swept away by floodwaters. They also dug two holes to cache a ton and a half (1.35 tonnes) of heavy supplies that they felt they could do without. The supplies were wrapped in animal skins and the hole was filled in again so no one could tell anything had been buried.

Lewis was seven miles (11.27 km) away from the Great Falls of the Missouri when he first heard their roar. He then knew they had chosen the correct branch of the river. When he got to the first of the five waterfalls that make up Great Falls, he sat and watched it for four hours. Lewis said it was, "the grandest sight I ever beheld." He wished his writing was good enough so that everyone would be able to know what he was seeing. Lewis sent Joseph Fields back to tell Clark that he had found Grand Falls.

Meanwhile, Clark was not having an easy time. He had "two men with the Tooth ake 2 with Tumers (boils), & one man with a Tumor & a slight fever." Sacagawea had gotten sick at the Marias River but was now critically ill. Clark wrote on June 10, "Sahcahgagwea our Indian woman verry sick I blead her." She became depressed and refused to take any medicine. They were worried that she might die, and it would be hard for little Pomp to survive without his mother. Lewis helped with Sacagawea's care when Clark's group reached the falls. She drank water from a sulphur spring and started to get better.

During the month they were at Great Falls they had some interesting and scary experiences, such as hearing distant explosions that they never could explain. An especially violent storm on June 29 brought hail so fierce that it knocked down and bloodied some of the men. Hail was frequent, and Lewis once measured hailstones that were seven inches (17.78 cm) around! Clark, Charbonneau, Sacagawea, Pomp, and York had made a trip to view the falls. They were in a deep ravine when they were nearly drowned by a flash flood. They lost many things in the flood, but the next day miraculously managed to find their important compass. Another time, Lewis had to jump into the river to escape a grizzly bear. He wrote about the grizzlies, "I must confess I do not like the gentlemen."

They discovered a giant spring which they called a "fountain." Today it is called Giant Springs and is one of the largest natural springs in the United States with 388 gallons (1466 liters) of water flowing into the Missouri River every day.

At Great Falls they hid their other pirogue among the willows. Lewis then tried out one of his inventions, a frame boat called the *Experiment*. This frame was to be covered with bark and caulked with pitch and then used as a replacement boat for the heavy boats they had to leave behind. Since there was no suitable bark, they covered the frame with elk and bison skins. Unfortunately, the boat leaked. Sadly Lewis wrote, "I therefore relinquished all further hope of my favorite boat." It was taken apart and buried and is probably still there. Without Lewis' boat, they had to make two dugout canoes. This was a challenge because they had to travel about thirty miles (48 km) to find large enough trees. They broke many axe handles and had to stop and whittle new ones. On one day, four men broke thirteen handles!

They celebrated the Fourth of July by some men hiking to the falls, and they had a dinner of beef, bacon, beans, and suet dumplings. Cruzat got out his fiddle and "they danced very merrily until 9 in the evening when a heavy shower of rain put an end to that amusement."

Portaging Around the Waterfalls and River Rapids

When Lewis and Clark arrived at the Great Falls, they could tell they wouldn't have an easy one-day portage, as the Hidatsas had led them to believe. The five waterfalls that make up Great Falls, and the dangerous rapids in between, make it impossible to travel by boat. A "portage" is needed when people are in a boat and they can't go any further on the water. They must get out and walk. A portage is carrying the boats and equipment overland until water is reached that can be traveled on again. It took a full month of backbreaking work to get around these waterfalls.

This portage ended up being one of the most difficult parts of the entire journey. It was an eighteen-mile (29-kilometer) uphill portage. Before they started, Lewis and Clark ordered everyone to go through their baggage and cache everything they didn't absolutely need. Then, from a cottonwood tree and the mast of the pirogue, they built a wagon frame on which they placed the canoes and remaining supplies. Even with the wagon it was very hard pulling it through ravines and over rocky ground without horses. The wagon broke and the wheels had to be remade. Several trips were needed to transport everything. They put double soles on their moccasins, but the prickly pear cactus stabbed their feet. Sometimes it was burning hot, but at other times, storms made the traveling even more difficult. Rain often turned the clay soil into a sticky "goo" that made walking almost impossible. They were so close to exhaustion that during brief rest stops they would fall asleep in a moment. Yet despite the hardships, Lewis reported that "no one complains, all go with cheerfullness." On one trip along the portage route some ingenious men even hoisted a sail over one of the wagons in order to take advantage of the wind. Lewis wrote, "This is really sailing on dry land."

People in recent times found out just how hard this portage was. Today's Great Falls, Montana, had a centennial celebration in 1984. A group of twenty-four men decided to reenact the portage, keeping as close to Lewis and Clark's route as possible and to use only the tools of that day. They had a very hard time. Their moccasins quickly wore out. The prickly pear cactus that had bothered Lewis and Clark was still just as much of a frustration. Sagebrush, bunch grass, thistles, and yucca also got in their way. They got very, very tired trying to pull the wagon.

Great Falls of Missouri Activity

To give you somewhat of a feel for what a portage is, create and play a portage relay. This relay should involve carrying "luggage" past an obstacle that is in your way. Be sure to think about how Lewis and Clark got around Great Falls and base your game on this history. For example, during part of your game you might want the players to have to hop, pretending that cactus spines are stabbing their feet through their moccasins.

1. Decide how your relay game will be played: rules, number of players, type of place where it should be played, how the game is won, how it relates to Lewis and Clark's portage at Great Falls, and so forth.
2. Get friends together to play your game.
3. After playing it, discuss how you could make your game better and what you liked about it. Make any necessary changes.
4. Play the game again, with the changes. Decide if you liked it better the second time and if any more changes need to be made. This game should give you a small feeling of what Lewis and Clark experienced at Great Falls.

Three Forks of the Missouri River

Entering the Rocky Mountains
July 15–29, 1805

The exhausted explorers put their eight canoes in the river above the falls on July 15. They had already used up half of the traveling season and had no idea how much further they had to go. As they traveled on up the Missouri River, it was obvious that they were entering real mountains. Lewis wrote on July 18, "saw a large herd of the Bighorned anamals on the immencely high and nearly perpendicular clift opposite us; on the fase of this clift they walked about and bounded from rock to rock with apparent unconcern where it appeared to me that no quadruped could have stood, and from which had they made one false step they must have been precipitated at least a 500 feet." The bison disappeared, but hunting was critical because it took a lot of meat to feed the group. That day they also passed a "handsome bold and clear stream we named in honor of the Secretary of war calling it Dearborn's river." They didn't realize this was the river the Hidatsas had told them about, a shortcut through the mountains to Lolo Pass.

At this point they were heading south and were very discouraged. It seemed that they were moving away from the mountains rather than getting closer. They were also baffled at not finding any Indians, although they had seen signal fires. All of a sudden, Sacagawea recognized her first landmark! Along a small creek were patches of white earth. At this place her people had collected material for white body paint. Lewis wrote on July 22, "The Indian woman recognizes the country and assures us that this is the river on which her relatioins live, and that the three forks are at no great distance. this piece of information has cheered the sperits of the party who now begin to console themselves with the anticipation of shortly seeing the head of the missouri yet unknown to the civilized world."

Clark and three men went on ahead. A small group could travel faster than the people who were with the canoes. They were also worried that the guns used for hunting would scare the Indians and make them think it was a war party. This small group might be able to meet the Shoshones before they got scared and ran away. Clark's feet were bleeding from the rocks and cacti, but his feet were no worse than anyone else's. He said he would rather tear them apart than freeze them off and that's what would happen if they didn't get over the mountains before it started snowing. In these high mountains, snow could start as early as August. Even Seaman's feet were sore. He was "constantly biting and scratching himself as if in a rack of pain."

Clark got to Three Forks on July 25. He left Lewis a note on a pole and set off to explore the rivers. He was sick with fever and chills but was determined to find the Shoshones so they could buy horses. Although he was exhausted, he fought off two grizzlies and rescued Charbonneau from drowning, but found no Indians. Lewis arrived and they stayed at Three Forks for several days to rest and to make new buckskin clothes.

Three Forks is exactly 2475 miles (3984.75 km) above the Mississippi River. The U.S. Geological Survey identifies this as the source of the Missouri River. Each of the three upstream rivers has a new name–the Jefferson, Gallatin, and Madison. The captains explored a short distance up each river and decided the branch from the southwest, the Jefferson, was most likely to take them to the Rockies.

On July 28 Lewis wrote, "Our present camp is precisely on the spot that the Snake [also known as Shoshone] Indians were encamped at the time the Minnetares [Hidatsas]. first came insight of them five years since. the Minnetares pursued, attacked them, Killed 4 men and 4 women a number of boys and made prisoners of all the females and four boys, Sah-cah-gar-we-ah our Indian woman was one of the female prisoners taken at that time. . . ." At last they had reached Shoshone country!

The Naming of Landmarks

Throughout their travels, Lewis and Clark gave names to rivers, creeks, mountains, and other physical features. As they started to travel into land where whites had not gone before, there were unlimited places that could be named. The Indians, of course, had names for these places, but at that time those were not recorded on the maps of the whites. Lewis and Clark named many of the physical features in today's Montana. (Over the years some of the places named by them have been changed.) There are many stories about how these places were named. Here are some examples.

In May of 1805, the expedition came to a large stream that entered the Missouri from the south. Clark "thought proper to call it Judieth's River" after Julia (or Judith) Hancock, a girl he later married.

Six men spotted a sleeping grizzly and decided to kill it. The more they shot at it, the more the bear charged. Eventually it was killed, but it had been a terrifying experience. They named a little creek near their camp "Brown Bear Defeated Creek."

One night a bison bull charged through their camp. People would have been crushed and killed if it hadn't been for the furious barking of Seaman. The bison ran off, but the closest creek was named "Bull Creek."

In June, Lewis named the "Marias River" after his cousin. He wrote, "I determined to give it a name and in honour of Miss Maria Wood called it Marias River. . . it is a noble river."

In July, the "Dearborn River" was named in honor of the Secretary of War. This was like repaying a favor. Henry Dearborn had let Lewis pretty much take what he needed to supply the expedition from the army supply depot at Harper's Ferry.

At Three Forks, Lewis wrote, "we called the S.W. fork Jefferson's River in honor of that illustrious personage Thomas Jefferson. the Middle fork we called madison's River in honor of James madison [Secretary of State] and the S.E. Fork we called Gallitin's River in honor of Albert Gallitin [Secretary of the Treasury]."

Three Forks of the Missouri River Activity

Like Lewis and Clark, you get to name some physical features. Below is a map that has no names on it. You decide what needs to be named and write the names beside those places on the map. Under the map, write the name of each place and tell why you gave it that name.

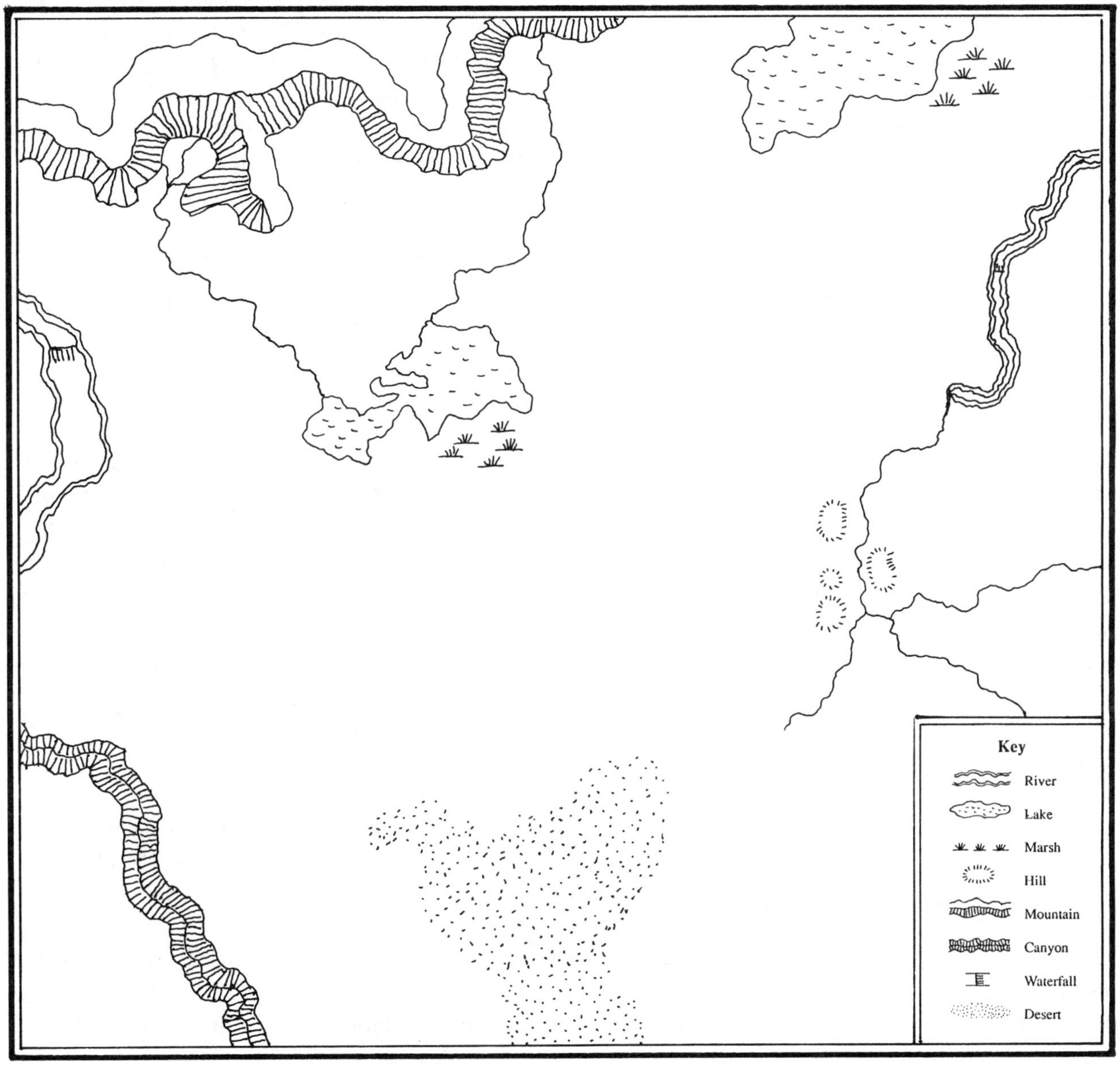

The Continental Divide

Between Three Forks, Montana, and Lemhi Pass, Idaho
July 30–August 12, 1805

They started out again July 30 following the Jefferson River, but many of the men were sick or hurt. Beavers were their latest problem! Their dams made it difficult to walk along the river bank. Then on August 1, Lewis took three men and began a new search for the Shoshone. Eventually, the Jefferson River split into two branches which confused them. He wrote a note to Clark, who was still with the canoe group, advising him to continue up the Jefferson River. The note was attached to a green willow pole beside the stream. Unfortunately, a beaver chewed down the pole with the note! Clark's group took the wrong turn. Drouilliard happened to be hunting in the area and found the lost group.

Near the Montana border with Idaho, the Jefferson River changes names and becomes the Beaverhead River. On August 8, Lewis wrote, "the Indian woman recognized the point of a high plain. . . which she informed us was not very distant from the summer retreat of her nation on a river beyond the mountains. . . this hill she says her nation calls the beaver's head from a conceived resemblance of it's figure to the head of that animal."

On August 9, Lewis set out with McNeal, Drouilliard, and Shields, determined to find the Shoshone. They were getting desperate and knew that having horses was the only way they could get over the mountains. The river again divided, but now the two streams were too small for canoes. That would be as far west as they would travel on the Missouri. At thc fork, Lewis left a note advising Clark to wait there until he returned. Lewis and his men followed a trail left by Indian horses along a creek. Much to their surprise, they saw an Indian on horseback, the first person they had seen since leaving today's North Dakota. For the next few minutes, Lewis' group and the Indian approached each other cautiously. As a peace sign, Lewis threw a blanket in the air three times. The Indian was suspicious, fearing a trap. Lewis was bitterly disappointed as the Indian turned his horse and disappeared into some willows.

They continued their search, following horse tracks along a stream up a mountainside. When the stream ended at a spring, Lewis was excited! He had reached the very source of "the Mighty Missouri in surch of which we have spent so many toilsome days and wristless nights. Thus far I have accomplished one of those grat objects on which my mind has been set for many years." (Geographers have decided the true source of the Missouri is Red Rock Creek, the fork they did not follow to the divide.) They crossed to the west side of the Lemhi Pass summit (7373' or 2247 m) on August 12, the first Americans to cross the Continental Divide. This divide is the long, high backbone of the North American continent that determines the direction water flows. Water flowing to the west would eventually reach the Columbia River and then flow into the Pacific Ocean. From the divide they could see the snow-covered mountains that seemed to go on endlessly to the west. It must have been discouraging. It would have also been exciting. Lewis and his men were stepping outside of the Louisiana Purchase, outside the United States.

Value of Horses

Lewis and Clark knew that they would not be able to cross the rugged Bitterroot Mountains without horses. They put all of their energy into finding the Shoshone Indians from whom they hoped to buy horses. Since the Shoshones were Sacagawea's own people, the language interpretation was much easier, and they were able to get their horses. Lewis felt that even though the Shoshones were rich in horses, they were poor people who often didn't have enough food. Except in emergencies, they would not kill and eat their horses because they had too much respect for them. Originally, they had probably gotten their horses from southern tribes such as the Utes and perhaps Comanches. The horses had helped them be a strong tribe on the plains. Once the Blackfeet, Hidatsas, and Sioux were able to get guns from British and French traders, the Shoshones were driven into the mountains. Lewis and Clark found that at that time, they dug camas roots and fished for salmon in the summer. When they were about to face starvation in the winter, they gathered their courage to go onto the plains to hunt bison. From the Nez Perce and tribes of the upper Columbia River, the expedition also exchanged for horses.

Horses have been very useful to people for thousands of years. They have provided an easy and fast way to travel across land. When the first Europeans came to North America, they found no horses. The American Indians didn't know about horses until the Spanish conquerors brought them to Mexico in 1519. Some of the horses of the Spanish and other explorers got left behind and became wild. The American Indians began to put these wild horses to good use around 1600. They used the horses for traveling, hunting, sport, and in battle.

In most countries today, the "iron horse" (train) and "horseless carriage" (automobile) have replaced the horse except for some recreational and work purposes.

The Continental Divide Activity

Research information about horses. Then put this information and some pictures on a colorful poster to share with others. These are some possible topics you may wish to use:

1. Kinds of horses
2. Body of the horse
3. Riding equipment
4. How to ride a horse
5. Care of a horse
6. Horse shows and sports
7. Raising and training horses
8. History of horses

Beaverhead River Forks and Lemhi Valley with the Shoshones

Clark Canyon Dam, Montana, to Tendoy, Idaho
August 13–31, 1805

As Lewis and his three men continued on, they finally met the Shoshones. They saw a man, two women, and some dogs. The people ran. Lewis tried to tie some gifts to the dogs, but they ran away too. They suddenly came upon two Indian girls and an old woman. They surprised the Indians who thought they were their enemy, the Blackfoot. They waited to face death bravely, but Lewis pulled up his sleeve to show his untanned white skin. They didn't know what a white man was, but at least he wasn't an enemy. Lewis gave them some gifts and painted their cheeks with vermillion, a sign of peace among the Shoshones. Drouilliard wrote, "After they became composed, I informed them by signs that I wished them to conduct us to their camp, that we were anxious to become acquainted with the chiefs and warriors of their nation."

On the way, they met sixty Shoshone warriors charging at full speed on horseback. The first Indians they had seen that morning had carried the alarm to the village. The Shoshones thought they were about to be attacked by their old enemy, the Blackfoot. Lewis dropped his gun and held up an American flag. The woman shouted to the chief that the strangers were friendly and held up the gifts. The chief dismounted, laid down his spear, and greeted Lewis warmly. The custom of these braves was to smear their faces with paint and bear grease. Lewis wrote on August 13, "these men advanced and embraced me very affectionately in their way which is by puting their left cheek to yours. bothe parties now advanced and we wer all carresed and besmeared with their grease and paint till I was heartily tired of the national hug. all the women and children of the camp were shortly collected about the lodge to indulge themselves with looking at us, we being the first white persons they had ever seen."

They were escorted to the Shoshone village which was really a nomadic camp. They met in a council lodge made of willow branches and leather hides. To show friendship, they smoked the peace pipe and took off their moccasins. In honor of their guests, the Shoshones celebrated most of the night. Lewis was given a piece of salmon so he knew for sure that these waters led to the Pacific Ocean. Gifts were exchanged. Lewis presented Cameahwait, their chief, with a Jefferson Peace Medal in appreciation of his hospitality.

Lewis asked for help in bringing the rest of his expedition over the divide to their village. The Shoshones were afraid to go back to the camp with Lewis. Strangers were usually considered to be enemies, and the Indians thought Lewis and his men might be leading them into some kind of a trap. They could be allies of the Hidatsas or the Blackfoot. Lewis challenged them, saying there must be at least a few brave warriors. Wanting to prove their courage and to receive gifts, eventually a group of men and women agreed to go. When Drouilliard shot a deer, the Indians hurried to the spot where he was cutting it up. They quickly grabbed the parts he was discarding, "like a parcel of famished dogs each seizing and tearing away a part of the intestens." This was the first meat the Shoshone had seen for days. Lewis aroused the Indians' curiosity by telling them they would soon meet a Shoshone girl who had been captured by the Hidatsas and see a man with black skin and curly hair. They were eager to see if this could be true.

Lewis was in a panic when he got back to the forks of the Beaverhead River where he had left a note for Clark six days earlier. (The note had been left on a dry, non-green stick that a beaver would not want!) Clark had not traveled that far up the river yet. The Indians thought they had been

tricked. Lewis was a quick thinker. First he gave the chief his gun, telling him that if there was trickery, the chief could shoot him. Lewis said a magic message from Clark would be found. Then he sent Drouilliard to get the note. Lewis pretended that the note, which of course the chief couldn't read, was from Clark. He pretended that it said that Clark was still coming up the river. By offering a knife and some beads, Lewis convinced some of the Indians to go with Drouilliard to meet Clark. This group eventually found Clark and the rest of the expedition slowly coming up the river.

Some remarkable reunions happened next. When Sacagawea saw the Shoshones, she became very excited. She showed that these were her own people by sucking her fingers, a sign to show "these are the people who nursed me." The Biddle translation of the journals described it (August 17), "a woman made her way through the crowd towards Sacajawea, and recognising each other, they embraced with the most tender affection. [She had been kidnapped at the same time as Sacagawea but had been able to escape.] Captain Clark went on, and was received by Captain Lewis and the chief, who after the first embraces and salutations were over, conducted him to a sort of circular tent or shade of willows. After this the conference was to be opened. Glad of an opportunity of being able to converse more intelligibly, Sacajawea was sent for; she came into the tent, sat down, and was beginning to interpret, when in the person of Cameahwait she recognised her brother. She instantly jumped up, and ran and embraced him, throwing over him her blanket and weeping profusely." It was an amazing coincidence that Cameahwait was Sacagawea's brother. She was so emotional about the reunion that she broke into tears from time to time and found it hard to translate. Even though Sacagawea could interpret, it was an awkward procedure. One of the captains spoke in English to Labiche. He spoke French for Charbonneau, who talked in Hidatsa to Sacagawea. She translated into Shoshone for Cameahwait. Sacagawea learned from Cameahwait that most of her family was dead.

Fortunately, the Shoshones had horses and mules. Trading for them, however, proved to be long and difficult. With Sacagawea as an interpreter, the captains told Cameahwait they needed horses and guides to cross the mountains. They explained the purpose of their trip and how it would help the Shoshones in the future. Once they had successfully completed their exploration, traders would follow bringing many wonderful things. Guns would be available for hunting and protection. After hearing this, the Indians became more interested and cooperative. (Lewis had seen twenty Indians chase ten antelope for two hours without getting one, so he knew the offer of guns would be appealing.) To obtain the first four animals, they had to barter a uniform coat, two pairs of leggings, a few handkerchiefs, four knives, and an old checkered shirt. For one horse, Clark gave up a pistol with a hundred balls, powder, and a knife. The Indians were about to leave on their annual bison hunt and had few horses to spare. The twenty-nine horses they eventually were able to buy were generally of poor quality.

Lewis hid the canoes by sinking them with rocks. In the ground he cached supplies they didn't need, plus his natural history collection for President Jefferson. He built saddles for the horses out of wood from empty boxes and canoe paddles. Lewis organized moving the supplies the forty miles (64.4 km) over the divide to the Shoshone village. By August 29, the entire group had moved over the divide and was ready to continue traveling.

Beaverhead River Forks and Lemhi Valley with the Shoshones Activity

On August 18, 1805, while the expedition was among the Shoshone Indians, Lewis celebrated his thirty-first birthday by catching trout. On that day he reflected in his journal, "This day I completed my thirty first year, and conceived that I had in all human probability now existed about half the period which I am to remain in this Sublunary world. I reflected that I had as yet done but little, very little, indeed, to further the hapiness of the human race or to advance the information of the succeeding generation. . . in future, to live for mankind, as I have heretofore lived for myself."

It must have been difficult for him to realize how important the information was that he was bringing back to the people of the United States. He *was* making a great contribution, but he couldn't see it on that day.

Think about your life and also think about the future. List some ways you could accomplish the things Lewis mentioned. These could be things you could do today and/or in the future:

- Further the happiness of the human race
- Advance information to the next generation

Lost Trail Pass and the Flathead Indians

Tendoy, Idaho, to Lolo, Montana
September 1–10, 1805

On September 1, with winter fast approaching, the expedition started traveling again. During their stay with the Shoshones, Clark and eleven men had taken a trip to explore the Lemhi River which flowed into the Salmon River. They had hoped to travel by river, but Clark found the route impossible. There were no trees big enough to make dugouts, and the rapids were too swift for canoes. The rockslide slopes were dangerous for people and horses, and game was too scarce to feed the group. Lewis also did some checking. He talked to the chief and wrote, "I now asked Cameahwait by what rout the Pierce nosed indians [Nez Perce] came over to the Missouri; this he informed me was to the north, but. . . that they had suffered excessively. . . I felt perfectly satisfyed, that if the Indians could pass these mountains with their women and children, that we could also pass them. . . ." With this information, they started out on a land route going north along the Lemhi River and then along the North Fork of the Salmon River. An old Shoshone warrior named Toby and his son agreed to guide them through the mountains.

This was their first experience in rugged, high mountain travel. It was a difficult route. Most of the horses were used to carry supplies rather than for riding. Clark wrote on September 2, "proceded on thro' thickets in which we were obliged to Cut a road, over rockey hill Sides where our horses were in perpeteal danger of Sliping to their certain distruction & up & Down Steep hills, where Several horses fell, Some turned over, and others Sliped down Steep hill Sides, one horse Crippeled & 2 gave out, with the greatest dificuelty risque &c. we made five miles & Encamped." Joe Whitehouse described it as being "nearly as steep as the roof of a house." They also had to drag their reluctant horses through deep bogs the men called the Dismal Swamp.

On September 3 Toby led them through the Lost Trail Pass. They crossed from today's Idaho back into Montana. Whitehouse wrote, "horrid bad going. . . we met with a great misfortune, in haveing our last Themometer broken, by accident." It was a severe loss considering the scientific purposes of the expedition.

The main range of the Bitterroot Mountains was still on their left. They had crossed an eastern part of it and then dropped down into Ross' Hole, a valley near today's Sula, Montana. Unexpectedly, they met a band of Flathead Indians. Clark wrote on September 4, "we met a party of the Tushepau nation. . . 400 Total and at least 500 horses, those people receved us friendly, threw white robes over our Sholders & Smoked in the pipes of peace." (Although they called them Tushapaws, they also called them Flatheads. They are not to be confused with the Indians of the Pacific Coast who used boards to flatten their heads.)

Lewis tried to learn as much about the country as he could from the Flatheads. He learned the awful truth that what had taken them fifty-two days to cover, they could have done in four if they had followed the Dearborn River. The group was able to buy thirteen horses and exchange seven of their worn-out animals for fresh ones.

After two days with the Flatheads, they headed north along the Bitterroot River. Aware that an even more difficult trail lay ahead, they took advantage of fair weather and camped beside a stream. They named it Traveler's Rest which is today's Lolo, Montana. There, they spent two days taking latitude readings, making moccasins, repacking and adjusting loads, hunting game (with limited success), and resting for the trip ahead.

Communicating Using Sign Language

When Lewis and Clark were among the Flatheads, they had a difficult time bargaining for horses because translations were difficult. The Flatheads spoke with gurgling, throaty sounds, in a language the captains had never heard before. The Flathead language was from the Salish family of Indian languages, common in the Pacific Northwest. This is why the language seemed so strange. They found a Shoshone boy living with the Flatheads who was able to translate to Sacagawea. She spoke in Hidatsa to Charbonneau, who spoke French to Labiche, who translated it into English for Lewis and Clark.

Communication was difficult when translations could be made. It was even harder, of course, when the only way groups could communicate was by sign language. However, a fairly common sign language developed among tribes in different regions. Sign language allowed hunters to "talk" to each other as they met on the bison ranges. Chiefs could reach agreements about trade or peace using sign language. Some members of the Lewis and Clark expedition knew this sign language and others learned it during the journey. For example, they learned that the name Flathead had nothing to do with the shape of the heads. Apparently it came from the sign language name for the tribe, hands pressed flat against either side of the skull.

Today, people who are deaf or who are communicating with them often use sign language. In this "manual method," sign language and finger spelling are used. Another method, the "oral method" uses speech reading (reading lips) and speech. A combined approach is most frequently used, using what is most appropriate for each person.

Thomas Hopkins Gallaudet graduated from Yale University in 1805. He became interested in teaching deaf people sign language, but there were no schools for the deaf in the United States at that time. He went to Paris, France, and studied their system of teaching at the Royal Institution for the Deaf. Gallaudet returned to the U.S. and with his friend, Laurent Clerc, opened The American School for the Deaf in Hartford, Connecticut, in 1817.

By learning sign language, the deaf can express thoughts quickly and completely. It is not a simple translation of English. It is a separate language with rhythms, meanings, and a beauty all its own. Signs are used to communicate words and ideas. Finger spelling is the hand spelling of each letter in a word. Each letter of the alphabet has its own sign made with the fingers and palms. It is slower than signing whole words and is usually used when very specific meanings are needed.

Angry

Beard

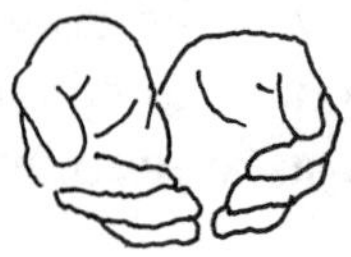

Bowl

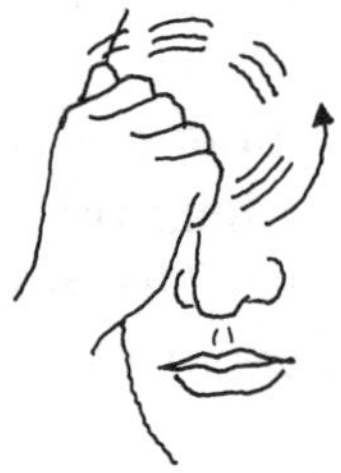

Crazy

Horse

Lost Trail Pass and the Flathead Indians Activity

Using the manual alphabet below, learn to sign your name and other words with finger spelling. Try to find someone to teach you to sign full words and ideas.

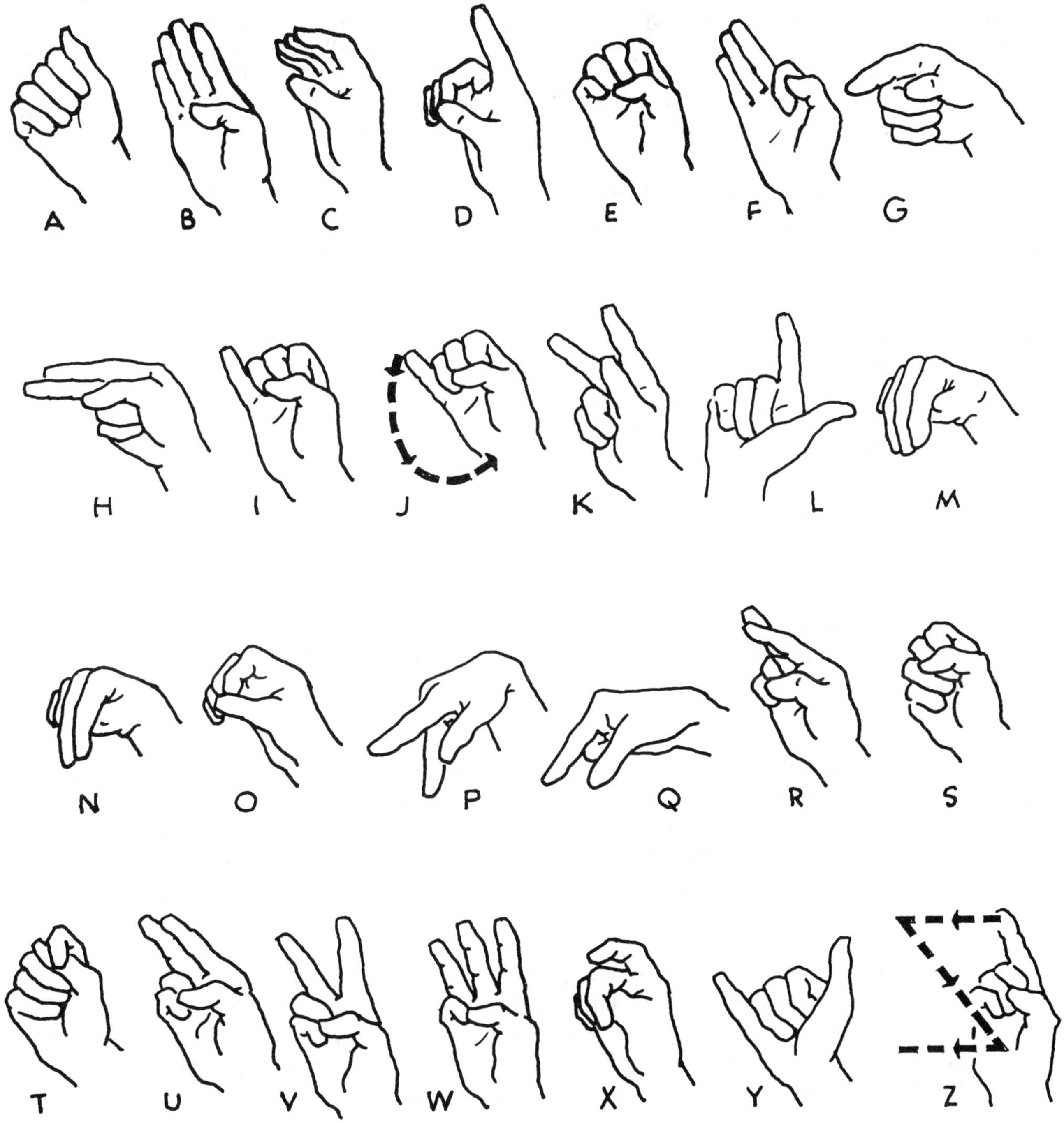

Crossing the Bitterroot Mountains

Between Lolo, Montana, and Weippe, Idaho
September 11–19, 1805

The crossing of Lolo Pass in the rugged Bitterroot Mountains was the worst time of crisis for the Lewis and Clark expedition. On September 12 Clark wrote, "The road through this hilley Countrey is verry bad passing over hills & thro' Steep hollows, over falling timber. . . Crossed a Mountain 8 miles with out water & encamped on a hill Side our hunters Killed only one Pheasent this afternoon. Party and horses much fatigued." They passed trees where Sacagawea showed them that starving Indians had peeled the bark in order to eat the moist fibers of the bark's inner layers.

The next day they got a delayed start because of looking for their horses that had strayed looking for forage. That day they found an astonishing thing, a hot spring. If they had not had to hurry on, they would have enjoyed the luxury of a hot bath! They passed beaver dams, but the hungry men saw no beaver.

By September 14 things were getting scary. Clark wrote, "here we were compelled to kill a Colt for our men & Selves to eat for the want of meat & we named the South fork Colt killed Creek, the Mountains we passed to day much worst than yesterday. . . ." Toby had accidentally led them off the main trail on the ridge and followed a side trail down to an Indian fishing camp on the Lochsa River. They found a brush fish trap but no fish.

The expedition had dropped down to 3000' (910 m). The only way out was to climb to 7000' (2133 m). Clark wrote on September 15, "We set out early and proceeded on over Steep points rockey & buschey as usial. . . Several horses Sliped and roled down Steep hills which hurt them verry much. . . when we arrived at the top we could find no water and Concluded to Camp and make use of the Snow to cook the remns. of our Colt & make our Super. Two of our horses gave out, pore and too much hurt to proceed." One horse that slipped was carrying Clark's field desk which held the expedition's notes. They scrambled to save the precious papers. The desk was smashed, but the horse survived.

In spite of these hardships, the captains continued to record their scientific observations. Some of the things they described were the common snowberry, western trumpet honeysuckle, and mountain huckleberry, Pacific mountain ash, three new species of grouse, varied thrush, Steller's jay, the gray jay and Lewis' woodpecker (named later for the captain), three species of fir, four species of pine, Sitka alder, western larch, Engelmann spruce, and western red cedar. Before this, many of these things were unknown to the scientific world.

Many of the men were depressed and growing weak with hunger. Three horses had been killed for food and that was all they could spare. Clark had seen a deer but couldn't hit it because his flintlock rifle had misfired seven times. Lewis wrote on September 18, ". . . this morning we finished the remainder of our last coult. we dined & suped on a skant proportion of portable soupe [brought from St. Louis]. . . a little bears oil and about 20 lbs. of candles form our stock of provision."

Things were getting so desperate that Clark and six men were sent ahead to find food. All they managed to kill was a stray horse. They ate some for breakfast and hung the rest on a tree for the group that followed. By September 18 Clark got a glimmer of hope. He wrote, ". . . from the top of a high part of the mountain at 20 miles I had a view of an emence Plain and leavel Countrey to the SW. & West. Encamped on a bold running Creek which I call Hungery Creek as at that place we had nothing to eate."

Mountain Survival in the Winter

Crossing the Bitterroot Mountains was a very dangerous time for the Lewis and Clark expedition. They faced the extreme hardships of little food, strenuous travel, an unknown route, and bitter cold. For many days they wrote about the severe cold and hard conditions. The following is one example:

On September 16 they awoke to snow covering their beds. Clark wrote, "began to Snow about 3 hours before Day and continued all day. at 12 oClock we halted on the top of the mountain to worm & indeed I was at one time fearful my feet would freze in the thin Mockirsons which I wore, we Encamped in a tickly timbered bottom which was scurcely large enough for us to lie leavil, men all wet and cold and hungary. Killed a second colt."

Crossing the Bitterroot Mountains Activity

People can die quickly from exposure in the cold, wet mountains. Lewis and Clark helped with medical emergencies throughout their journey. What first aid should they have used to treat these medical emergencies?

1. **frostbite**: Frostbite results when crystals form in the fluids and underlying soft tissues of the skin. It is the most common injury resulting from exposure to the cold. Usually, the frozen area is small. The nose, ears, cheeks, fingers, and toes are most commonly affected. As frostbite develops, the skin changes to white or grayish-yellow. Sometimes there is pain at first. Blisters may appear later. The affected part feels very cold and numb. The person is often not aware of frostbite until someone else observes the pale, glossy skin. As time passes, more serious conditions can develop.

2. **cold exposure**: When the body temperature drops to an abnormally low level, this is known as *hypothermia*. Exposure to extreme cold for a lengthy time can produce shivering, numbness, low body temperature, drowsiness, and muscle weakness. This is life threatening.

Imagine that you could go back in time and join the Lewis and Clark expedition for the climb through the Bitterroots. You would still have the same horses, but if you could take supplies and clothing that are available today, what would you take for yourself and the others to make this journey easier and safer? (Don't forget Sacagawea, Pomp, and Seaman!)

Among the Nez Perce Indians

Weippe to Orofino, Idaho
September 20–October 6, 1805

Clark and his men were extremely relieved when they left the hardships of the Bitterroot Mountains and entered the valley of the Clearwater River and found the Nez Perce Indians. Clark wrote, "proceeded on through a butifull Countrey for three miles to a Small Plain in which I found maney Indian lodges. at the distance of 1 mile from the lodges, I met 3 Indian boys, when they saw me they ran and hid themselves in the grass. I desmounted gave me gun and horse to one of the men [and] gave them Small pieces of ribin & Sent them forward to the village. Soon after a man Came out to meet me, with great Caution & Conducted me to a large spacious Lodge [made of woven mats] They call themselves Cho pun-nish or Pierced noses. the fiew men that were left in the Village and great numbers of women geathered around me with much apparent signs of fear. those people gave us a Small piece of Buffalow meat, Some dried Salmon beries & roots all of which we eate hartily. I find myself verry unwell all the evening from eateing the fish & roots too freely." (Chopunnish was the phonetic spelling of the name these Indians had for themselves. Nez Perce, or "pierced noses" is the name given them by French traders who later visited them. Some wore brass rings in their noses.)

Clark traded trinkets for food and sent it back into the mountains with Reuben Fields for Lewis' group. When they arrived in the village two days later they became ill from the diet of fish and roots too. The change in diet from bison, to nothing, and then to dried fish and camas roots caused them all to have stomach disorders and diarrhea. There may also have been a bacteria in the dried salmon to which the Nez Perce had developed an immunity but caused the explorers to become sick. The bulb of the camas lily was a main food of the Nez Perce. It was either eaten raw, steamed, or pounded into a flour to be made into soup or bread. Sergeant Gass thought it tasted like pumpkin. They tried to get some meat back in their diet. They shot a few deer and also began buying and eating fat Indian dogs. (Except for Clark, most of them grew to enjoy it.)

The expedition moved from the village to an island in the river to meet friendly Twisted Hair. He apparently was the ranking chief while the other leaders were away with a war party. Clark described him as "a cheerful man of about 65 with apparent siencerity." Lewis and Clark held a council, explaining their mission and presenting medals and gifts of friendship. They left an American flag for the chief who was away. They were eager to learn about the country ahead. They found that this was where they should start traveling by river again. They could float down the Clearwater to the Snake and on to the Columbia River and the Pacific Ocean. On September 26 Lewis and Clark set up a camp at the confluence of the North and Main forks of the Clearwater River, 5 miles (8 km) west of today's Orofino. They called this Canoe Camp. Those who were not sick built canoes from ponderosa pine or red cedar.

They left their thirty-eight horses with relatives of Twisted Hair who promised to take care of them until the explorers returned. Remembering that the horses were property of the U.S. Army, Lewis had them branded "U.S. Capt. M. Lewis." (The branding iron was found almost a century later on an island in the Columbia River.) The Indians kept their promise. In fact, one night Lewis and Clark secretly cached some powder and their saddles, to be picked up on their return trip. Later, a flood exposed the secret cache, but the Indians rescued the goods and held them until the expedition returned.

Mapmaking

Lewis and Clark were eager to learn about the land beyond the Nez Perce camps. Clark wrote on September 22, "I got the Twisted hare to draw the river from his camp down which he did with great cherfullness on a white Elk skin. . . ."

The expedition was grateful for the maps and travel information they got from the Indians. Sometimes, however, it was hard to know how accurate it was. The Indians had no compasses. They did not measure distances in miles or kilometers but in "sleeps" or "suns." The amount of ground they covered during one "sun" depended on the pace of their horses. There was also the frustration of trying to communicate when so many interpreters were needed. The Indians often drew rough maps, either on hides or on the ground. They would use something sharp like a stick to scratch out rivers and add little heaps of sand to show mountains. Directions and landmarks were shown fairly accurately, but distances were hard to determine. For example, they thought the Hidatsas had told them that the portage around the Great Falls would be just a simple half-mile (.8-km) long, rather than eighteen miles (29 km).

During the days of Lewis and Clark, there were few maps of what is today the western United States, and those that did exist were very incomplete. Those maps were not very accurate because so little exploring had been done by the mapmakers. Much of what Clark did on the trip was to map the regions they were passing through. President Jefferson had asked Lewis and Clark to make maps, hoping that others would be able to use the maps to follow the best route west. For example, when they were traveling by river, Clark sketched the winding route and took notes on what he saw. He often measured the widths of rivers and recorded waterfalls, rapids, and important landmarks. The two captains combined their notes and gradually a map of their journey was developed.

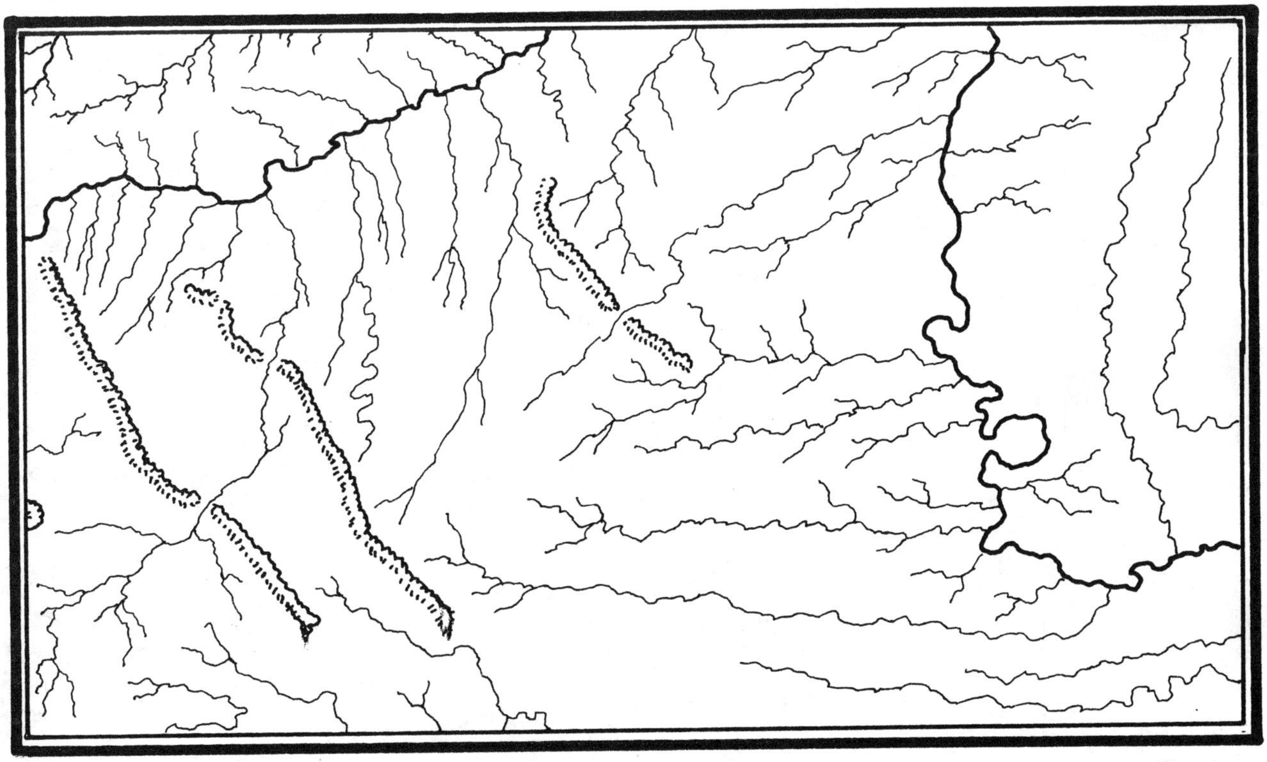

Among the Nez Perce Indians Activity

Make a map to show how to get from one place to the other. Draw a map from your home to your school. Try to draw it to scale.

1. Start by drawing a rough map, one that basically shows the route but is not accurately drawn to scale.
2. Then have someone drive the route with you. Have this person help you figure the odometer readings. Then write these amounts down for each section of the map.
3. Redraw the route accurately. You need to decide your scale of miles (or kilometers). The scale you choose depends on how big you want your map to be.
4. Be sure to draw an arrow for "north" on your map. North is usually at the top of maps. If you don't have a compass you can tell which way is north because the sun rises in the east. Therefore, if the sun is ahead of you in the sky in the morning, north is to your left side.
5. Once you have the route drawn, name and/or draw points of interest along the way, such as your house, your school, street names, a favorite park, and so forth.
6. If you want your map to look old, prepare the paper in this way before you put your final copy of the map on it. Draw your map on white paper with a sharp pencil. Paint all over the paper with a watery mixture of yellow and brown paint. Let it dry. Trace over your writing with a thin-tipped black felt pen. With help from an adult, burn the edges of the paper. This is done most safely outside. Light a candle and stick one edge of the paper in the flame. Burn just a little of the edge. Blow out the burning paper, being sure it's out on the top and the bottom. Then burn a little more. Continue in this way until the entire edge of the paper is burned. Glue your map on black construction paper. Let any curled edges stick up, rather than being glued down flat.

Canoeing the Rivers of the Inland Empire

Orofino, Idaho, to The Dalles Dam, Oregon, and Washington
October 7–23, 1805

"The morning of the 7th was pleasant, and we put the last of our canoes into the water; loaded them and found that they carried all our baggage with convenience. We had four large canoes; and one small one. . ." wrote Gass. Twisted Hair and a lesser Nez Perce chief named Tetoharsky volunteered to guide them to the Columbia River.

They set off down the Clearwater River. This was the first time they found a river flowing the direction they were going, but these western rivers were very swift. Clark wrote on October 8, "Sprung a leak. . . [canoe] Split open and Bottom filled with water & Sunk, the men, Several of which Could not Swim hung on to the Canoe." The next day their Shoshone guides disappeared without their pay, perhaps afraid of the rapids or they might have been uncomfortable around the Nez Perce. The Clearwater joined the Snake River, and then it was on to the Columbia River. The forests of pines disappeared and the land became more "barren and broken," as their journals described.

On October 16 Clark wrote, ". . . proceeded on Seven miles to the junction of this river and the Columbia. . . we halted above the point on the river to smoke with the Indians who had collected there in great numbers to view us, great quantities of a kind of prickley pares, much worst than any I have before seen." The Indians lived in lodges made of woven grasses rather than in tipis. These Yakima (Sokulk) Indians welcomed them. Clark wrote more on October 16, "we purchased for our Provisions Seven dogs, Some fiew of these people made us presents of fish. The 2 old chiefs precured us Some fuil Such as the Stalks of weeds or plants and willow bushes. one man made me a present of about 20 lb. of verry fat Dried horse meat." All the expedition's salt was gone now and the tasteless fish diet grew so boring that they eagerly accepted dog meat stew from the Indians. Lewis felt that dog meat was better than horse meat. "While we lived principally on the flesh of this animal, we were much more healthy, strong and more fleshey than we had been since we left the Buffaloe country." During the times of little food, no one ever considered eating Seaman!

On October 19, Clark and two men traveled ahead to a small village. Despite the efforts of the Nez Perce guides, the Indians were terrified of the white men and hid in their lodges. Clark shot a crane and a duck which fell from the sky. The Indians had not seen guns before so they thought the travelers "came from the clouds and were not men." Clark entered one of the lodges and found thirty-two frightened people crying and wringing their hands. He took each person by the hand and offered trinkets and bits of ribbon, and they calmed down a bit. However, when it seemed that he magically lit a peace pipe with his magnifying glass, their terror returned. When Sacagawea arrived, her presence calmed them, and they smoked the peace pipe.

They arrived at the spectacular Celilo Falls on October 22. Here, the powerful Columbia roared its way through the volcanic Cascade Mountains in a series of waterfalls and rapids. At Celilo Falls they had to portage their canoes and supplies. They lowered their canoes on elk skin ropes. Friendly Indians helped by carrying the heavy supplies on horseback. During the days of Lewis and Clark, Celilo Falls was the most impressive waterfall on the Columbia. This was the Indians' traditional fishing grounds where they speared fish or scooped them up with long-handled nets. They stood on wooden platforms and rocks to catch the salmon as they jumped the falls on their way to their spawning grounds. This type of fishing continued until 1957 when The Dalles Dam was built and the lake behind the dam flooded Celilo Falls.

Life Cycle of the Salmon

Lewis and Clark learned the role salmon played in the lives of the Indians along the Columbia River and its tributaries. It was the foundation of their diet. Clark wrote, "The women in the village heated rocks and used them to boil water in woven baskets. They cooked the fish in the boiling water and served them on small, woven mats." Clark was amazed at the great amount of salmon available. One old Indian boasted that there were so many fish you could walk across the Columbia on their backs without getting your moccasins wet! He observed that they dried salmon on scaffolding, pounded it, and then packed it in baskets to trade with other tribes.

Where the Clearwater River met the Snake River, Lewis and Clark observed the end of the seasonal salmon run, where the fish return from the ocean to their home stream. Salmon are born in a freshwater stream, then spend part of their lives in the ocean. Usually in the early summer of their most mature year, they head back to their home stream. They stop feeding as they enter the fresh water and live off their stored body fats. The salmon struggle for weeks to get back upstream. They often have to face waterfalls, dams, pollution, predators, and other obstacles. If they survive and get back to where they were born, the female digs a nest in the gravel and lays thousands of eggs. The eggs are fertilized by the male. The female covers the eggs with gravel. This process is called spawning. Within a short time, the salmon die and the bodies drift downstream. Clark observed that the river was filled with dead and dying fish and wrote, "Those [salmon] which was offered to us [by Indians] we had every reason to believe was taken up on the shore dead [so] we thought proper not to purchase any, we purchased forty dogs [to eat] for which we gave articles. . . such as beeds, bells & thimbles."

Canoeing the Rivers of the Inland Empire Activity

How salmon find their way to their home stream in order to spawn is a mystery to scientists. It is known that smell plays a part, but it is probably more complex than any one thing. Try the following activity to help remember the end of the life cycle of the salmon. Prepare the following, and then do the activity with your friends.

1. Get two paper or plastic cups (not clear). Place a wadded-up paper towel in one cup. Pour a small amount of a safe liquid on the paper towel. This liquid needs to have a fragrance. Examples might include mint extract, vanilla, soy sauce, or vinegar. Place the second cup on top of the first, with the rims together. Place masking tape around the rims, sealing them together. On the bottom of one cup write the name of a river. If it's a real name it should be a river that salmon live in, such as the Columbia. On the bottom of the other cup, poke a few small holes so the fragrance can be smelled. Don't tell anyone what's in the cup! Prepare at least three set of cups, with different river names and fragrances.
2. Gather your friends and tell them about the life cycle of the salmon. Explain how studies have found that the smell of rivers plays a part in helping a salmon find its home stream so it can return to spawn. Have your friends "become salmon." Assign them to certain cups. Have them learn the names of their rivers and smell the fragrances. Send them out of the room. Rearrange the cups. When the salmon "swim back in," they should smell all the cups, without looking at the names of the rivers, and find their home streams.
3. You can play this several times with some variations: Since not all salmon live long enough to spawn, when the friends come back in, some can be pulled aside and told that they didn't survive. Tell an example of something that could have happened to them, such as being eaten by a bear, caught by a trawler, or killed by fertilizers that washed into the river. These hazards could be from their time in the ocean or in the river. You can also fool the salmon. When they are out of the room, spray the inside of one cup with a room deodorizer to change the fragrance. Retape the cup. The salmon will have trouble finding the home stream because of their river being "polluted."

The Columbia Gorge

The Dalles to Cascade Locks, Oregon
October 23–November 2, 1805

Below Celilo Falls, the Columbia River flows in a gorge between steep basalt cliffs, increasing its volume and power. Lewis and Clark named these dangerous rapids the Short and Long Narrows. At the Short Narrows they decided to risk taking their canoes through the fierce rapids. Clark wrote on October 24, "The whole of the Current of this great river must pass. . . thro' this narow chanel of 45 yards wide as the portage of our canoes over this high rock would be impossible with our Strength. . . I thought by good Stearing we could pass down Safe. . . notwithstanding the horid appearance of this agitated gut swelling, boiling & whorling in every direction. . . we passed Safe to the astonishment of all the Inds. who viewed us from the top of the rock." With winter so close, they took chances they normally would have avoided. Clark admitted, "we should make more portages if the season was not so far advanced and time precious with us."

After running the rapids, the expedition took time to rest at a site they called Rock Fort. The area was a favorite fishing ground for the Wishram and Wasco Indians. Clark observed that their main food was dried and pounded fish, and he counted "107 stacks. . . in different places on those rocks which must have contained 10,000 lbs of neet fish." This was a busy trading area. For example, the Nez Perce came to trade their furs, hides, bear claws, bear grass (used to make baskets), and dried meat for dried clams, tools whittled out of wood, cloth and metal items from white traders who came by ship to the mouth of the Columbia, and highly valued dentalium shells. The Wishram village had twenty-one plank longhouses, the first wooden town the expedition had seen since starting their journey.

It was discovered the Wishrams were feared by the Nez Perce guides. The captains expressed Jefferson's wish that all Indians live together in peace. They gave medals and other gifts of friendship and danced to Cruzatte's violin music. On October 25, Twisted Hair and Tetoharsky left the expedition, explaining that they could be of no further service because they did not understand the language of the tribes down the river. Clark wrote that they stopped work to smoke "a parting pipe with our two faithful friends, the chiefs who accompanied us from the head of the river."

They next faced the rapids of the Long Narrows which looked very dangerous. The captains ordered all the men who could not swim to go ashore. They carried the most important baggage, the guns, ammunition, papers, and instruments. The rest of the men took the canoes, in pairs, through the swirling water.

About twenty miles (32 km) west of today's The Dalles, the amount of rainfall increased, and the vegetation changed. At this point, Lewis and Clark left the dry Inland Empire and entered a densely forested area. Clark wrote, "after brackfast we proceeded on, the mountains are high on each side, containing scattering pine white Oake & under groth, hill Sides Steep and rockey: Here the mountains are high on each side. . . has Some Snow on them at this time. more timber than above and of greater variety." They saw what they thought were large buzzards, but were really California condors. They explored Memaloose Island, Klickitat for "Land of the Dead." It was a site of an Indian burial ground. Clark wrote, "I saw 8 vaults for the Dead. the bones in some wer 4 feet thick. . . maney wooden gods. . . ."

Volcanic Peaks of the Cascade Mountains

As Lewis and Clark's expedition canoed down the Columbia River toward the Pacific Ocean, they observed the spectacular volcanic peaks of the Cascade Mountains on both sides of the river. On October 19 Clark wrote, "I descovered a high mountain of emence hight covered with Snow, this must be one of the mountains laid down by Vancouver, as seen from the mouth of the Columbia River. I take it to be Mt. St. Helens." He had mistaken this for Mt. Adams. The British expedition of Captain George Vancouver in 1792 named Mt. Hood, Mt. St. Helens, and Mt. Rainier. When Clark did see Mt. St. Helens, he wrote, "we had a full view of Mt. Helien which is perhaps the highest pinical in America. This is the mountain I saw on the 19th of October last covered with Snow, it rises Something in the form of a Sugar lofe." (It no longer is "pinical" in shape. It lost the upper 1300' [396 m] of its 9667' [2947 m] on May 18, 1980, when it erupted.) Clark had copies of Vancouver's maps with him, and he could now check their accuracy and add his own observations. On the return trip up the Columbia, Clark named one of the peaks Vancouver's expedition had not named. He named it Mount Jefferson in honor of Thomas Jefferson who had sent them on their journey.

The Cascade Mountains stretch the entire length of Washington and Oregon and extend into British Columbia to the north and into California to the south. It has taken over fifty million years of geologic unrest, violence, erosion, and climate changes to create the Cascade Mountains. The volcanic peaks did not all develop at once. Some were old and deeply eroded by the time the younger mountains were formed. Volcanoes occur in places where the earth's crust is weak. Hot, melted rock called lava from deep in the earth boils up and bursts through the weak spot.

The Indians of the Columbia River have many legends about the mountains. One of the best known involves Mt. St. Helens, Mt. Adams, and Mt. Hood. As one version of the legend goes, many years ago there was a natural bridge across the Columbia River above where Lewis and Clark named the rapids the Great Shute. Today this is known as the Cascades of the Columbia. At the center of the natural bridge was a sacred flame that was tended by a beautiful young maiden named Loo-Wit. The two sons of the supreme being, Wy'East and Klickitat, had fallen in love with the maiden and began quarreling so violently over her that their father decided to teach them all a lesson. He destroyed the natural bridge, and the rocks fell into the river, turning a six-mile (9.7-kilometer) stretch of the river into the dangerous rapids. He changed the two men into mountains on opposite sides of the river. Wy'East became Mt. Hood and Klickitat became Mt. Adams. Loo-Wit became Mt. St. Helens.

The Columbia Gorge Activity

Make a model of a volcano that can really erupt.

1. In a shallow baking pan, place an empty soda bottle. Mold clay around the sides of the bottle so it looks like a mountain. (You could also use plaster of Paris, soil, or sand.) Be sure to leave the hole in the top of the soda bottle uncovered. This opening is like a volcano's crater. It is the place where the lava comes out.
2. Fill the bottle almost to the top with warm water. Add some red food coloring and five or six drops of liquid detergent. Add about two tablespoons of baking soda. Then pour vinegar into the bottle until suds begin to rise out of the top of the bottle and flow down the sides of the model in an "eruption." It might need to be stirred. Note: When baking soda and vinegar are mixed together, they form carbon dioxide, a bubbly gas. These bubbles mix with the soap and come pouring out of the top of the volcano like lava.
3. Write an Indian-style legend to go with your erupting volcano.

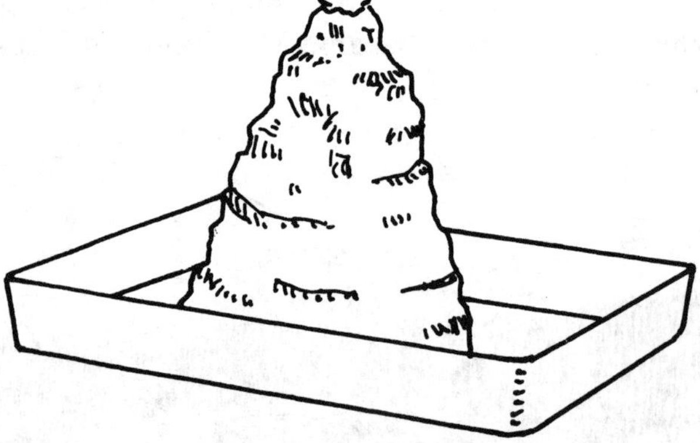

Along the Columbia to the Pacific Ocean

Beacon Rock to Cape Disappointment, Oregon, and Washington

November 2–24, 1805

At massive Beacon Rock on November 2, they reached tidewater. Here, the height of the Columbia River was affected by Pacific Ocean tides. They observed "Great numbers of Sea Otters" and thought they were near the ocean, but it was over 100 miles (161 km) away. On November 7 at Gray's Bay, Clark wrote, "Great joy in camp we are in view of the Ocian, this great Pacific Octean which we been so long anxious to See." The ocean can't be seen from there, but with bad weather and high waves, they thought they had arrived. They still had another twenty miles (32.2 km) to go.

Clark was fascinated with the way the Indians in this area made themselves beautiful. He wrote, "Their noses are all Pierced, and they wear a white shell. . . pushed thro' the nose. all the women have flat heads pressed to almost a point at top. They press the female childres heads between 2 bords when young untill they form the skul as they wish which is generally verry flat. This amongst those people is considered as a great mark of buty, and is practised in all the tribes we have passed on this river more or less." The Indians of this area lived in houses thatched with straw and covered with bark. They introduced the expedition to the "roundish roots about the Size of a Small Irish potato which they roasted in the embers until they became Soft, This root they call Wap-pa-to."

The weather was so bad that it was a struggle to travel the last few miles (kilometers) of the Columbia. They camped at several miserable locations. The following are some of Clark's journal comments: ". . . the Seas roled and tossed the Canoes in such a manner this evening that Several of our party were Sea Sick." ". . . our party all wet and cold. . . " "A Tremendious wind. . . Lightineng and hard claps of Thunder, and Hail. . . rained with great violence. . . our Situation is dangerous." ". . . eleven days rain and the most disagreable time I have experienced. . . I can neither git out to hunt, return to a better situation, or proceed on. . . ." "The rain. . . distroyd the robes and rotted nearly one half of the fiew clothes the party has, perticularley the leather clothes. If we have cold weather before we can kill & Dress Skins for clothing the bulk of the party will Suffer. . . ."

They camped at today's Baker Bay for ten days. Here, they really first saw the Pacific Ocean. On November 16 Clark wrote, "It is now apparent that the sea was at all times too rough for us to proceed further down the bay by water. We therefore landed, and having chosen the best spot we could select, made our camp of boards from the old Chinook villages." They found the village "deserted by the Inds & in full possession of the flees." Since they were camped along the river, Lewis and Clark each took groups to explore the nearby ocean. During one hike, Reuben Field shot a condor with an amazing wingspan of $9^1/_2$ feet (290 cm). Earlier, Clark noted that they "saw great numbers of waterfowl" and complained that "I could not sleep for the noise kept by the Swans, Geese, White & black brants Duck. . . & sand hill Crane, they were emencly numerous and their noisie horrid."

They had been exploring the north side of the Columbia for a location for a winter camp. Clark wrote, "They [Chinooks] generaly agree that the Most Elk is on the Opposit Shore added to this a convenient Situation to the Sea coast where we Could make Salt, and a probibility of Vessels comeing into the Mouth of Columbia from whome we might precure a fresh Supply of Indian trinkets to purchase provisions on our return home; together with the Solicitations of every individual, except one of our party, induced us to Conclude to Cross the river and if a Sufficient quantity of Elk could probebly be precured to fix on a Situation as convenient as we could find." Since this was a military expedition, it was unusual that every member of the group got to vote.

Northwest Coast Indian Art

When Lewis and Clark left the Nez Perce, they traveled in the five dugout canoes they had made. They found the western rivers to be very swift and dangerous and soon wished they had larger, sturdier canoes. Along the Columbia River Gorge, Clark wrote, "I observed on the beach near the Indian Lodges two butifull canoes of different Shape & Size to what we had Seen above wide in the middle and tapering to each end, on the bow curious figures were cut in the wood &c. Capt. Lewis exchanged our Smallest canoe for one of them by giveing a Hatchet & few trinkets to the owner. . . these canoes are neeter made than any I have ever Seen and calculated to ride the waves, and carry emence burthens." The expedition desperately needed seaworthy boats when they got to the windswept waters near the ocean. It was hard enough paddling, even with their larger canoes. For example, on November 8 Clark wrote, "after Dinner we took the advantage of a returning tide and proceeded on. . . here we found the Swells or Waves to high that we thought it imprudent to proceed; we landed unloaded and drew up our Canoes."

These Indian canoes were decorated in the traditional Northwest Coast style. On November 4 Clark noted beautifully fashioned seaworthy canoes and wrote, "I counted 52 canoes on the bank in front of this village maney of them verry large and raised in bow." These canoes often held fifty or more paddlers and could transport large amounts of freight and people in the roughest currents and seas.

Northwest Coast Indian art is a very old style. It is a very precise art form, made of specific shapes that, when connected and combined, create a whole design. Look at pictures of Northwest Coast Indian art to see ways these shapes are connected. The shapes are often carved first and then painted. The largest and most frequent of the painted shapes look like this:

Ovoid **U Form** **Example: Whale**

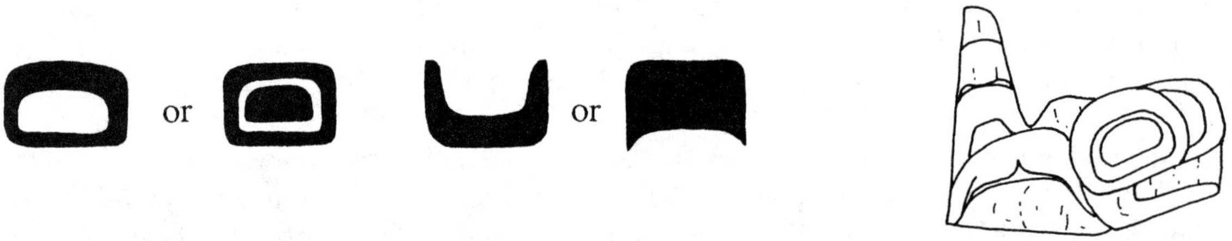

These designs are still painted today. They are usually painted in red and black. Sometimes a third color is used. A blue-green color can be added if it is between red and black, not used as an outline. White spaces are left too. By 1920 the Indians began using paint bought from stores. Before this, the paint pigments came from a variety of sources. In the early days, salmon eggs were dried and then chewed. This saliva solution was mixed with the pigment. They made black paint from ground charcoal. The red paint came from clays, the inner bark of the hemlock tree, or Indian paint fungus. Greens and blues came from copper ores or clays stained with the oxide. White came from ground shells, bones, or white clay. To correctly paint the colors, note that when the *U* is black, the inside is red. When the ovoid is black, the inside is black.

Along the Columbia to the Pacific Ocean Activity

Draw a large Northwest Coast Indian-style canoe. Draw and color designs in this Indian style on the bow of the canoe. Below your picture, write a paragraph describing the symbols you used. These should be nature-related symbols but of your own creative design.

Example:

Winter at Fort Clatsop

Astoria to Cannon Beach, Oregon

November 25, 1805–March 22, 1806

It wasn't easy for Lewis and Clark to get from the Columbia's north shore to the south shore where they hoped to build their winter fort. It took twelve days because the weather was so bad, and their canoes were not built for such rough conditions. They had to canoe back upriver seventeen miles (27 km) before they found water calm enough to cross.

The site they found for the fort was located about ten miles (16 km) west of today's Astoria. Here, wood was plentiful, there were more deer and elk, tall trees protected them from the fierce storms, and they were close to both the ocean and the Columbia River. Although they were very tired, on December 8 they started working long hours in the rain and cold to get the fort built. The stockade was fifty feet (15 meters) square with two rows of rooms facing each other across a twenty-foot (6-meter)-wide parade ground. They were able to move in on Christmas Eve.

On Christmas morning the captains were awakened by gunfire. Rifles were fired to celebrate the holiday, plus shouts, cheers, and songs. The captains gave tobacco to those who smoked and silk handkerchiefs to the others. Clark wrote that he received "two Dozen white weazils tails of the Indian woman," and other gifts were also exchanged. Their Christmas dinner was almost inedible. Clark wrote, "We would have Spent this day the nativity of Christ in feasting, had we any thing either to raise our Sperits or even gratify our appetites, our Diner concisted of pore Elk, so much Spoiled that we eate it thro' mear necessity, some Spoiled pounded fish and a fiew roots." They missed their families and friends, and the rainy weather added to their misery.

Fort Clatsop was named for the friendly local Indians. The Clatsops, Chinooks, and Cathlamets often visited the fort to trade. Since no nation had a clear claim to this land and since there were so few trading supplies left, the captains did not have their usual Indian councils. The Indians were friendly, but the captains realized how outnumbered they were and established strict rules to protect the safety of their people and supplies.

There was little excitement during the winter. Lewis' journal often said, "Not any occurrences today worthy of notice." However, everyone stayed busy. The men spent a lot of time hunting, but there was not a lot of game. In this damp climate, the meat spoiled before it could be brought to the smokehouse. They were able to buy some smelt from a Clatsop chief. They found these fish delicious, but they spoiled unless quickly smoked. They were so oily that the Indians would put a wick through a dried end in order to use it as a candle, so they became known as a candlefish. Elk skins were made into new clothes, blankets, and 358 pairs of moccasins. When Lewis complained that his men didn't have enough brains to tan their hides, he meant that the only way they had of preparing the hides was by rubbing the brains of the animals into the hides to make them soft. Guns and equipment had to be repaired. Dried roots and berries were stored in empty flour sacks. When their supply of tallow candles ran out, they used their candle molds to make new candles from elk fat.

During the winter they had time to catch up on their journal writing. They worked by candlelight at their stand-up desks. Lewis wrote pages of descriptions and drawings of the local plants and animals. Clark copied Lewis' observations into his own journal because Jefferson had asked for duplicate records in case one set should get lost. Clark worked on a detailed map of their route to the Pacific and planned their return trip. Their descriptions of the lives, languages, and customs of the coastal Indians are among the best ever written. They were important because most of the Indians were dead twenty years later due to smallpox and malaria.

Lewis and Clark had hoped that when they reached the Pacific they might find a ship exploring the coast. They wanted to buy trading goods for their return trip. They also hoped to send one or two members of the expedition home by sea, taking a copy of the journals. Unknown to the men, the *Lydia*, a ship from Boston, had visited the mouth of the Columbia in November to trade and buy furs.

The winter passed slowly with storms bringing heavy rains, fog, and winds. During the 106 days they stayed at Fort Clatsop, it rained every day except twelve, and there were only six clear days! The entries in Clark's weather journal for January were usually, "Sun visible for a fiew minits" or "rained verry hard last night." The dampness gave nearly everyone rheumatism, colds, and "enfluenzy." Clothing rotted and fleas infested their bedding and their clothes. The men stood in the rain to try to wash the fleas away!

By March they were getting eager to head east. They wanted to report their findings to Jefferson. They couldn't start so early that there would be snow in the mountains or so late that the Missouri River would freeze before they could reach St. Louis. They hoped to get their horses from the Nez Perce before the Indians set out over the mountains for their spring bison hunt. They were also eager to go because they had experienced too much rain, too little food, homesickness, and general depression. They were worried about having enough food for the trip and not having enough trade goods left to trade for food. There were so few fishhooks, beads, small knives, little files, burning glasses, and trinkets that they could all be wrapped in two handerkerchiefs. At least they would be heading home. Clark carved his name in a pine tree and added, in case they failed to make it back, "By Land from the U. States in 1804 & 1805."

After they left, the fort soon decayed. Five years later a fur trapper found only a pile of logs where the fort had stood. In early 1900s the site was located by old-timers who had seen pieces of the foundation when they were young. In 1955 the Oregon Historical Society built a full-size replica of the fort by following a floor plan Clark had sketched on the elk skin cover of his journal. Since 1958 the fort has been operated by the National Park Service as the Fort Clatsop National Memorial.

Making Salt at a Salt Cairn

The Lewis and Clark expedition had used all of its salt and needed to make more. They needed it for their health, to keep meat from spoiling, and to improve the taste of their often-spoiled meat and fish. During the winter at Fort Clatsop they had time to make salt.

On December 28 five men took "5 of the largest kittles" and walked five days in cold rains to locate a salt-making site. They found a good site about fifteen miles (24 km) south of the fort at today's Seaside. Clark wrote on January 7, ". . . the Salt Makers had made a Neet close camp, convienent to wood Salt water and the fresh water of the Clatsop river." It was also near the friendly Clatsop and Killamox (Tillamook) Indians.

They built a "furnace" of rocks and built a fire underneath. This was called a salt cairn. They placed the copper kettles on top of the rocks and boiled seawater over a slow fire. When the water evaporated, the dry salt lined the kettles and could be scraped into kegs. It was cold, hard work. They kept the fire burning, carried the seawater, and often got sick from the wet conditions. When some of the men took a sample back to Fort Clatsop, Lewis wrote, "they commenced the making of salt and found that they could obtain from 3 quarts to a gallon a day; they brought with them a specemine of the salt of about a gallon, we found it excellent, fine, strong, & white; this was a great treat to myself and most of the party." The men returned to the fort with twenty gallons (38 l) of salt on February 21. It was packed into twelve small kegs and carried on the trip back east with them. Today, a replica of the salt cairn has been constructed to show the public how Lewis and Clark's salt-making process worked.

Winter at Fort Clatsop Activity

To grow salt crystals, do the following:

1. Fill a glass jar with hot water. Add salt as long as it keeps dissolving.
2. Tie one end of a string to a paper clip for a weight and tie the other end to a pencil. The string should be long enough to reach the bottom of the jar. Drop the string into the hot solution. Place the pencil across the top of the jar.
3. Let the solution cool slowly. Watch it for several days. Watch the growth of your salt crystals. Look at the shape of the crystals under a microscope or magnifying glass.

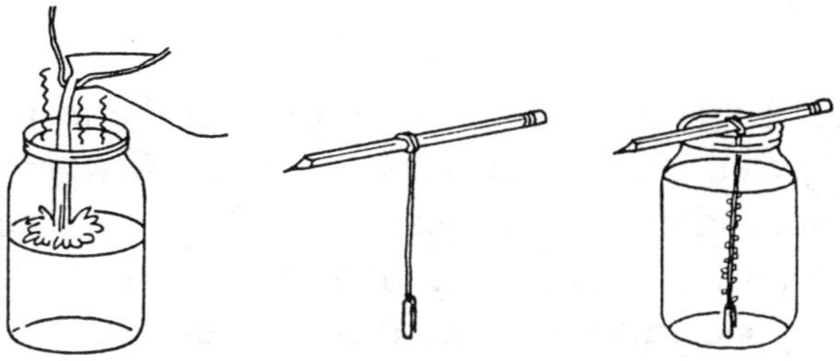

For a variation on this activity, try the following:

1. Dissolve about an ounce (29.5 ml) of table salt in a half pint (480 ml) of boiling water.
2. Pour the solution into a shallow pan. Place a string in the solution and over the edge of the dish.
3. Let the solution evaporate slowly for a day or two. Look at the crystals in the pan and along the string. Notice how these crystals differ from the ones you made in the first activity. Think of reasons for the differences in the salt crystals.

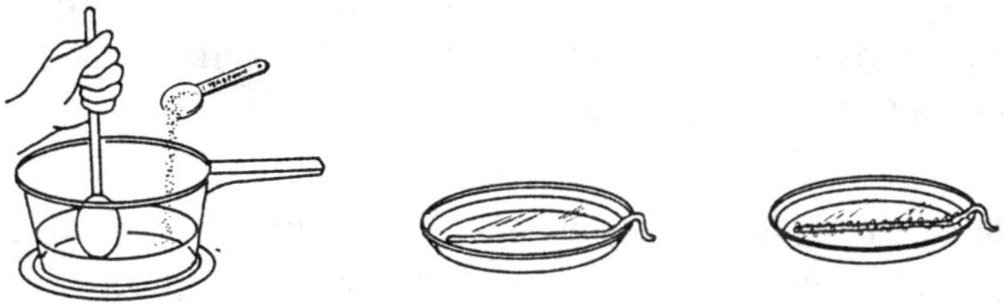

Lewis and Clark didn't have sugar that winter, but sugar crystals can be grown in a similar way to salt crystals. Do the following:

1. Prepare the glass, pencil, string, and paper clip in the same way as described above.
2. Boil $^3/_4$ cup (180 ml) of water in a saucepan. While the water is boiling, carefully stir in granulated sugar, a little at a time until no more will dissolve. This will take about 2 cups (480 ml) of sugar.
3. Carefully pour the solution into a glass. If you put a silver spoon into the glass as you pour, it will absorb enough heat to keep the glass from cracking. Remove the spoon. Put the glass where it won't be disturbed. In about a week, crystals will form. Keep letting the crystals grow until there is rock candy on the string.
4. Compare these sugar crystals with the salt crystals you grew.

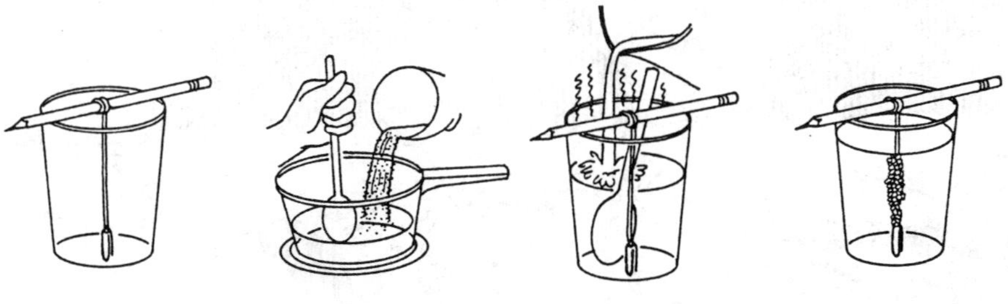

Trading for Whale Blubber and Oil

While at Fort Clatsop, the expedition learned of the beaching of a whale about eight miles (13 km) south of the salt cairn. Clark took a group of fourteen to see the whale. They knew that fried blubber and roots cooked in whale oil would be highly nourishing. Lewis wrote on January 6, "Charbono and his Indian woman were also of the party; the Indian woman was very importunate to be permitted to go, and as therefore indulged; she observed that she had traveled a long way with us to see the great waters, and that now that monstrous fish was also to be seen, she thought it very hard she could not be permitted to see either." They went first to the salt cairn and then over Tillamook Head to the beach.

Clark wrote on January 7, "I hired a young Indian to pilot me to the whale. we proceeded on under a high hill which projected into the ocian about 4 miles. My guide made a Sudin halt, pointed to the top of the mountain and made signs that we could not proceed any further on the rocks, but must pass over that mountain. I hesitated a moment & view this emence mountain to top of which was obscured in the clouds. I soon found that the path become much worst as I assended, and at one place we were obliged to Support and draw our selves up by the bushes & roots. after about 2 hours labour and fatigue we reached the top from which I looked down with estonishment to behold the hight which we had assended which appeared to be almost perpendicular." This mountain was Tillamook Head, a high (1136 feet [346 m]) rocky headland that jutted out in the Pacific. Lewis named this headland "Clark's Point of View" because of Clark's enthusiasm for the view. Today this is Oregon's popular Ecola State Park.

On January 8, one of their few clear days, Clark wrote, "from this point I beheld the grandest and most pleasing prospect which my eyes ever surveyed, in my frount a boundless Ocean. . . the Seas rageing with emence waves and breaking with great force."

Clark wrote about the rest of the hike on January 8, "Wind hard. . . if we had unfortunately made one false Step we Should eneviateably have fallen into the Sea and dashed against the rocks in an instant, fortunately. . . arived on a butiful Sand Shore and proceeded to the place the whale had perished, found only the Skelleton of this Monster the Whale was already pillaged of every Valuble part. this Skeleton measured 105 feet. I returned to the Village on the creek which I shall call E co-la or Whale Creek." The whale was near the mouth of Ecola Creek in today's Cannon Beach. The Indians were boiling the blubber in large wooden troughs. The animal's bladders and intestines served as containers for the oil, which the Indians traded with "great reluctiance and in small quantities only." With "utmost exertion" Clark succeeded in purchasing about 300 pounds (135 kg) of whale blubber and a few gallons of oil. This was the farthest point of the entire Lewis and Clark expedition.

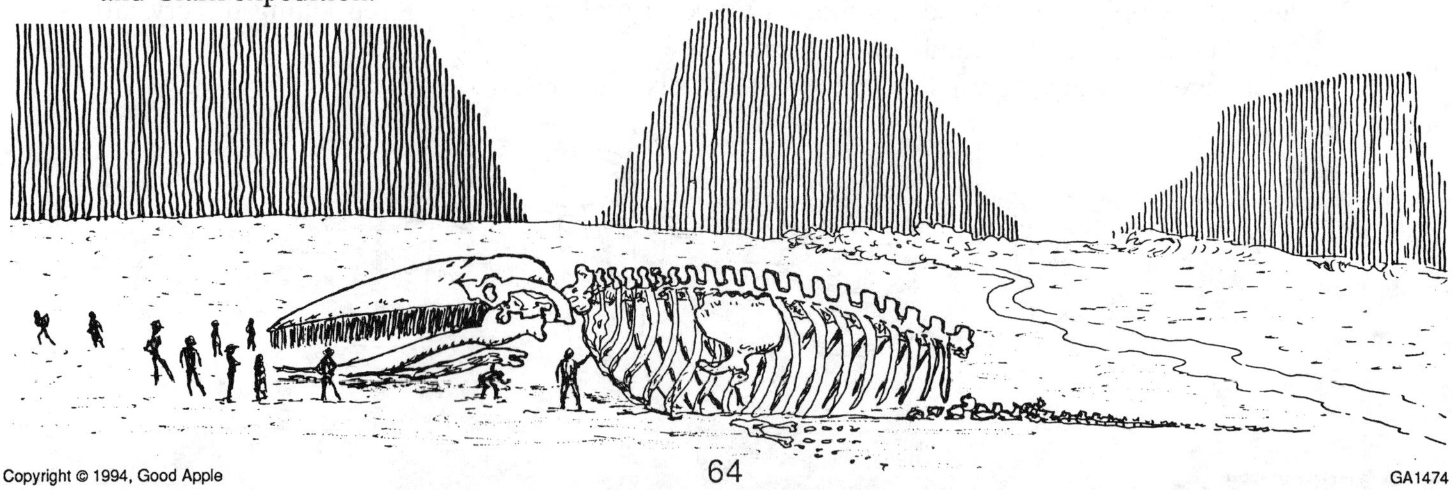

Winter at Fort Clatsop Activity

Using a stiff cookie dough, sculpt the skeleton of a whale.

1. The following recipe or a similar type may be used.
2. Research what the skeletons of different types of whales look like. Choose one to make.
3. Recipe:

   3 egg whites
   1 $^3/_4$ cups (.42 l) sugar
   $^1/_2$ teaspoon (2.5 ml) baking powder
   $^1/_2$ teaspoon (2.5 ml) grated lemon peel
   1 $^1/_2$ cups (.36 l) chopped, blanched almonds
   1 $^3/_4$ cups (.42 l) flour

   Beat until smooth the egg whites, sugar, baking powder, grated lemon peel. Mix thoroughly with the almonds and flour.

   Flour hands lightly. Shape bones. Spread on a greased baking sheet. Bake at 375° F (191° C) for 10 to 12 minutes or until the dough is light brown. These are hard cookies, meant for dunking in milk or juice.
4. Compare whale skeletons to those of other animals.

Return Trip Along the Columbia River

Fort Clatsop, Oregon, to Wallula Gap, Washington
March 23–April 29, 1806

The homeward journey began on a rainy March 23. Clark wrote, ". . . loaded our canoes & at 1 P.M. left Fort Clatsop on our homeward bound journey. at this place we had wintered and remained from the 7th of Decr. 1805 to this day and have lived as well as we had any right to expect." They started to canoe back up the Columbia River.

They heard from Indians that the salmon run was late and there was little food upstream. The expedition was worried because they knew they would need to trade with the Indians for food. They decided to stop for a few days to hunt and dry as much meat as possible and to gather hides that could be used in trading. They camped at the mouth of the Sandy River (which they called the Quicksand River). They learned from some visiting Indians that they had missed finding the Willamette River and Valley. On April 2 Lewis wrote, "several canoes of the natives arrived at our camp. . . We redily prevailed on them to give us a sketch of this river which they drew on a mat with a coal. . . Capt. Clark determined to return and examine this river."

Clark backtracked with a group of seven members of the expedition and an Indian guide to explore the Willamette River (which the Indians called "Multnomah"). They apparently traveled not quite as far as today's downtown Portland. Clark recognized the potential of the valley. Clark wrote, ". . . appears to possess water enough for the largest ship. It is in fact the only desirable situation for a settlement on the western side of the Rocky mountains, and, being naturally fertile, would, if properly cultivated afford subsitance for 40,000 or 50,000 souls." (By 1843, the fertile Willamette Valley had begun to draw pioneer settlers.)

On the return trip they mentioned the many spectacular waterfalls along the Columbia Gorge, which they hadn't mentioned on the trip west so the weather must have improved. They had to struggle against the strong current of the Columbia. Water from the spring thaw had swollen the river twelve feet (3.65 m) higher than the fall and increased the force of the rapids. The portages were again tiring, and they had to pull the canoes upstream with towropes. Past Celilo Falls they were able to trade their beads and canoes to Indians for horses. It took a great deal of bargaining, but at least they could then travel overland.

They accepted the hospitality of Chief Yellept and camped with the Walla Walla tribe from April 27 to 29. Lewis called the Walla Wallas "the most hospitable, honest, and sincere people that we met with in our voyage." These friendly Indians provided a lavish feast. Cruzatte played his fiddle, Indians drummed, and the Walla Wallas, Yakimas, and whites danced together until early in the morning. Yellept gave them much-needed food and ferried the expedition and their horses to the south side of the river. The Walla Wallas sold them several horses so they then had twenty-three. Yellept gave Clark a beautiful white horse and told the captains about the overland shortcut to the Nez Perce. A day after they left, the helpful chief even sent three men riding after them to return a steel trap they had forgotten.

Seaman, Lewis' Newfoundland Dog

One of the faithful members of the Lewis and Clark expedition was Seaman, Lewis' dog. He was a large, black Newfoundland breed. In July 1803, before the journey started, Lewis went to Pittsburgh to get the boats he had ordered. When he arrived, the boats were not done. It is believed that during the delay, Lewis made friends with Seaman, the boat builder's dog. The boat builder was often drunk and mistreated the dog. When Lewis paid for the boats, he also bought Seaman. Lewis wrote about his dog in 1803, ". . . one of the Shawnees. . . offered me three beverskins for my dog with which he appeared much pleased. the dog was of the newfoundland breed, one that I prised much for his docility and qualifications generally for my journey and of course there was no bargain. I had given 20$ for this dogg myself."

Seaman had many adventures during the trip, but one of the scary times was on the group's return trip, about two hundred miles (322 km) up the Columbia. Some of the Indians who had been friendly in the fall were now hostile. Rocks were thrown, and there were a few scuffles. The patience of the expedition was running low. At one point, some Wahclellah Indians lured Seaman away, perhaps as a toll for passing up the river. To Lewis it seemed like theft. Lewis wrote, "three of this tribe of villains. . . stole my dog this evening, and took him toward their village; I was shortly afterwards informed of this. . . by an indian who spoke the Clatsop language and sent three men in pursuit of the theives with orders if they made the least resistence or difficulty in surrendering the dog to fire on them. . . they overtook these fellows or reather came within sight of them. . . the indians discovering the party in pursuit of them left the dog and fled." This was the first time on the entire trip that such a command had been given against the Indians. Jefferson had insisted the Indians be treated "in the most friendly & conciliatory manner which their own conduct will admit." This was how seriously Lewis took the stealing of his dog! The next day the chief apologized for "two very bad men" that weren't representative of his people. He helped guard the expedition and was given a medal as a reward.

Seaman was a good hunter. When he saw many gray squirrels swimming across a river, he jumped in, caught and killed one, and brought it back. Lewis wrote, ". . . observed a number of squirrels swimming the Ohio. . . I made my dog take as many each day as I had occation for. . . I thought them when fryed a pleasant food. . . he would take the squirrel in the water, kill them and swiming bring them in his mouth to the boat." It was a good thing he was able to help the hunters, because he ate as much as any one man!

The trip wasn't always easy for Seaman. When they portaged around the Great Falls, thorns got in Seaman's feet and made them bleed. At times he could not walk. Lewis made him a set of rawhide boots to protect his paws. Wood ticks gnawed on his ears. In order to make them feel better, Clark rubbed his ears with bear grease. Many nights he howled in pain. Seaman even survived a beaver attack! Clark wrote, "we came to a Beever house. Capt. Lewis's Dog went in and drove them out." This was very risky. Lewis wrote, "one of the party wounded a beaver, and my dog as usual swam in to catch it; the beaver bit him through the hind leg and cut the artery; it was with great difficulty that I could stop the blood; I fear it will yet prove fatal to him."

Seaman was a helpful guard at night. Lewis wrote, "our dog gives us timely notice of their [bear's] visits, he keeps constantly padroling all night." He also warned them when a bison nearly stampeded through their campsite, trampling them to death. Another time, they were camped on a sandbar in the middle of the river. Seaman saved the expedition from drowning by awakening them in the middle of the night because the river was rising. Since Seaman was so smart, he played a part in the peace councils with the tribes. Besides Lewis showing off his air gun and York showing his feats of strength, Seaman performed.

During his return trip, Lewis had given the name Seaman's Creek to a northern tributary of the Blackfoot River in today's Powell County, Montana. (This is now known as Monture Creek.) The naming of this creek was a mystery to historians for years. They could not figure out who Seaman was. Finally, after carefully looking at the poor handwriting in the journals, they realized that this was the name of Lewis' dog. Before this, historians had thought his name was Scannon. The name Seaman makes sense because Newfoundland dogs have long been associated with water and helping fishermen. This breed has webbing between their toes, thick coats of coarse and oily hair, broad chests with large lung capacities, and are excellent swimmers. Since they are often called "sea dogs," the name "Seaman" was very appropriate for Lewis' dog.

The last journal mention of Seaman was on July 15, 1806, near the Great Falls of the Missouri. Lewis wrote that "my dog. . . howls with the torture he experiences from them [mosquitoes]." Even though he wasn't written about after this, he was such a loved and valued member of the expedition, he probably survived the entire trip. If he had had any further difficulties, surely someone would have written about it!

Return Trip Along the Columbia River Activity

Imagine what Seaman must have thought about during the journey with the Lewis and Clark expedition. He survived dangerous situations, participated in the hunts, saw new and different lands, met many Indian tribes, suffered hardships of bad weather and lack of food, and was a great help and companion to the expedition.

Write a story about one day of the expedition from the point of view of Seaman. Pretend you know what the dog was thinking and doing. This needs to be written in a "historical fiction" style where the story is based on real history, but some of the details are fiction. Write it as if it really could have happened in the way it is described. Draw and color a picture of Seaman to go with the story.

Returning to the Nez Perce and Bitterroots

Wallula Gap, Washington, to Lolo, Montana
April 30–July 2, 1806

The expedition left the Columbia River and traveled east. Along the way they were met by the friendly Nez Perce. The expedition was very hungry, but it had been a hard winter, for the Indians only had cous roots to spare. Since their trading goods were almost gone, the captains cut off the buttons from their few remaining coats and traded them for the little food they could get. They were excited when the Indians brought Clark a horse bearing Lewis' own brand. It was one they had given to Twisted Hair for safekeeping. On May 8 they set out with a chief named Cut Nose (a nostril had been slit in battle) to find Twisted Hair and their other horses. The two chiefs got in an argument over how the horses had been cared for. Lewis and Clark managed to help the chiefs settle their differences, and all but two of the horses were returned.

On May 10 they moved on through a spring snowstorm to the village of Broken Arm, the principal chief of the Nez Perce. He had been away when they visited before. The American flag that he had been sent in the fall was standing outside his house. Lewis wrote, "The village of the broken arm consists of one house or Lodge. . . built in the usual form of sticks mat and dry grass. it contains twenty-four fires and about double that number of families. . . the noise of their women pounding roots reminds me of a nail factory." Since several important chiefs had ridden there to see them, Lewis and Clark had a peace council with the Indians.

The expedition moved its camp to the Clearwater River near today's Kamiah, Idaho. They had to remain for almost a month waiting for the mountain snows to melt. Lewis wrote of "that icy barrier which separates us from my friends and country." They built a brush and grass shelter and used this time to make saddles and ropes. They ran races to build up stamina for the mountain hike. Lewis studied the grizzly bear and named it for the "grizzled" appearance of its fur which gets lighter near the tips.

They had hoped to have the Indians guide them over the mountains, but the Nez Perce were afraid of being attacked by the Blackfeet and Hidatsas. The expedition felt it could wait no longer for guides, so they set off June 10 to find their own way. It was spring at the lower elevations, with fields of camas lilies, but in the mountains they found twelve to fifteen feet (3.6 to 4.5 m) of snow. They knew they would never be able to follow the trail. There was no choice but to turn back. Lewis wrote, "the first time. . . on this long tour that we have ever been compelled to retreat." They cached some baggage and food on a scaffolding and headed back to a meadow that was free of snow.

Five Nez Perce guides were eventually found. Lewis and Clark were grateful to their guides as they moved as fast as they could along steep cliffs in seven feet (2.13 m) of snow. On June 29 they crossed Lolo Pass and were over the Bitterroots. They camped near a hot springs where they bathed, probably for the first time in months. The next day they reached Traveler's Rest, their former camp. There was now plenty of game, and they were able to rest for two days. They decided to split into three groups for part of the return trip. Although it was dangerous to have smaller groups, they felt it was their duty to explore as much of the area as they could for President Jefferson. Lewis admitted that he "could not avoid feeling much concern on this occasion."

Medical Practices During the Expedition

Throughout the expedition, Lewis and Clark both practiced medicine. They were not trained doctors, but they had enough background to help the expedition and the Indians. No doctor was taken on the trip because army regulations allowed only one "surgeon" to each forty-five men. Lewis had learned some medical knowledge from his mother, Lucy Meriwether Marks, who was famous for her skill in using herb remedies. He also had a crash course in medicine from Dr. Benjamin Rush when he was in Philadelphia preparing for the trip. (Dr. Rush was the first professor of chemistry in the U.S. and was one of four doctors who signed the Declaration of Independence.) Their medical practices may seem strange today, but they were the common treatments at that time. The captains often wished they had more medical training. To avoid harming anyone with improper treatment, they said they always took "care to give them no article which can possibly injure them." Although they did not know it then, one of the common "medicines" they used was mercury, which is now known as a poison.

When Joseph Fields got a snakebite during the early part of the trip, Clark wrote that "Capt. Lewis bled him. . . ." The treatment for most illnesses included "bleeding" the patient. They made a cut and allowed the "bad blood" to flow out. At that time, they did not know about bacteria or viruses so bleeding seemed logical. Also, a mixture of Peruvian tree bark and gunpowder was placed over the wound, and it was lit with a flame.

When their supply of trade goods became low, they often traded medical treatment for the things they needed. Indians along the Columbia often had eye irritations. The captains thought it might have been caused by fine sand or the glare of the sun on the water where the Indians fished. The captains mixed their own "eye water" from ingredients in their medicine chest. Among the Nez Perce, Clark had gained a reputation as a healer when they visited in the fall. On the return trip, as many as fifty sick Indians flocked to him each day. Lewis wrote, "My friend, Captain Clark, is their favorite physician. . . ." The wife of a chief had an abscess on her back which Clark thought was beyond help. The Indians insisted he open the infection and treat it. She started to recover at once so the grateful chief gave Clark a horse which they ate immediately.

William Brattan had been in great pain. They gave him a "sweat." He sat over a pit lined with hot rocks. He was covered with blankets and drank mint tea while water was poured over the rocks to make as much steam as he could stand. After each sweat, he was "taken out and suddonly plunged in cold water twise and was then immediately returned to the sweat hole." Miraculously, the next day he walked free of pain! They gave a similar sweat to a paralyzed Indian who regained the use of his arms and legs.

Returning to the Nez Perce and the Bitterroots Activity

Medical practices were different in the days of Lewis and Clark. Make a chart comparing medical practices in the early 1800s and today. (This can be a comparison with just the Lewis and Clark expedition or with the 1800s in general.)

Medical Problem	1800s Practice (or Lewis and Clark)	Today's Practice
Example: Baby Pomp had difficulty cutting his baby teeth. (Pomp's face swelled, he had a high fever, and an abscess behind an ear.)	Poultice of wild onion and cream of tartar, plus a mixture of pine resin, beeswax, and bear's oil (Poultice is a hot, soft, moist mass put on a sore or an inflamed part of the body.)	Cold teething ring and an aspirin-free liquid drop painkiller in a child's dose

Lewis' Return–Blackfoot Country

Lolo, Montana, to Below Little Knife River, North Dakota
July 3–August 12, 1806

Lewis, with nine men and the five Nez Perce guides, set off on July 3 to explore the northern route. Lewis would take a shortcut to the Great Falls and then head north to explore the Marias River before returning to the Missouri River. The next day, the Nez Perce guides were ready to return home. Lewis wrote, "smoked a pipe with these friendly people and at noon bid them adieu." He gave the brother of Chief Cut Nose a small peace medal and a gun. The man was so pleased that he gave Lewis his most precious possession, the gift of his own name, White Bearskin Folded.

They crossed the Continental Divide at what is now called Lewis and Clark Pass. After months of little food, they were delighted to find bison again. Lewis was amazed that "there were not less than 10 thousand buffaloe within a circle of 2 miles." (Note: The correct name is bison, not buffalo. True buffalo are found only in Asia. According to a Blackfoot legend, the bison came from a great hole in the ground. When the fifty million bison were hunted to near extinction, many Blackfeet believed that the whites had found the hole, driven the bison back in, and plugged it up. By 1900 only twenty bison were known to exist.)

By July 13 they arrived above the Great Falls. It had taken eleven days to reach this spot from Travelers Rest. The year before it had taken two months, plus six hundred extra miles (966 km) to travel the same distance. When they opened their cache, they found it had been flooded. The bearskins and all the plant specimens Lewis had collected and dried with such care were ruined. An important chart of the Missouri was safe and other articles could be dried out. The mosquitoes were so numerous that the men often inhaled them and even Seaman howled. There were many grizzlies in the area. Hugh McNeal's horse almost rode over a hidden bear, throwing him. He clubbed the bear over the head with his gun. McNeal spent several hours in a tree waiting for the angry bear to leave.

Lewis took Drouillard and the Field brothers to the Marias River. Sergeant Gass and the others would wait at the Great Falls for part of Clark's group. They would portage the Great Falls, get their cached supplies, and then go to the mouth of the Marias to meet Lewis. It was important to explore the Marias River because the Louisiana Purchase was to include all land drained by the Missouri River. They hoped this tributary of the Missouri would be far to the north because then much of the rich fur country would belong to the United States, not England. Clouds hid the stars and kept Lewis from getting an accurate latitude reading. He wrote, "The morning was cloudy and continued to rain. . . which I now call camp disappointment." It was obvious, however, that the river did not extend as far north as he had hoped.

They started back toward the Missouri on July 26. Near Two Medicine Creek, Lewis and his men saw eight Blackfeet Indians of the Piegan tribe. He gave them gifts and his usual peace council, and they camped together that night. The next morning there was a struggle as the Indians tried to steal their guns and horses. In the process, two Indians were killed. The Blackfeet fled, leaving many of their horses and weapons behind. Lewis picked out four of the best Indian horses and burned their bows, arrows, and shields on the campfire. This was the only warfare on the trip. The incident would affect Blackfeet/white relations for years.

Lewis was worried that the Indians would seek revenge. The four men rode 120 miles (193 km) in a little more than twenty-four hours. It was good timing because not long after they reached the Missouri River, they found the rest of their group floating down the river in the five canoes and white pirogue. They quickly opened the caches left at the mouth of the Marias River. Things were in fair condition, but the red pirogue was too decayed to repair. The horses were freed, and they set off down the Missouri, eager to leave the Indian danger behind and meet Clark's group at the Yellowstone.

At the mouth of the Yellowstone on August 7, they found a note left by Clark, explaining that he had moved downriver because hunting was poor and the mosquitoes were bad. Lewis' group continued down the river. They spotted a herd of elk on an island and stopped to hunt. Peter Cruzatte, who had poor eyesight, fired at a movement in the grass that he thought was an elk. He had really shot Lewis, his commanding officer, in the thigh! The wound gave him a high fever, and he could barely move because of the pain. On August 12 Lewis described one last plant, the pin cherry. His wound was so painful that he stopped writing in his journal and left it to Clark for the rest of the trip. On that same day, a few miles below the Little Knife River, Lewis and Clark's groups met back together.

Preserving History Through Art

In the days of Lewis and Clark, there weren't cameras. Many of the early explorers took artists along to record what these new lands looked like–the Indians, animals, plants, rivers, mountains, and so forth. Although Lewis and Clark did some sketching in their journals, they weren't trained as artists and the number of sketches was quite small. Some historians feel that one of the mistakes Jefferson made in planning the expedition was not including an artist. Later, painters George Catlin and Karl Bodmer retraced part of the Lewis and Clark expedition. Unfortunately, some of the things Lewis and Clark saw had changed a great deal by the time these artists got back to those places. Much knowledge had been lost.

George Catlin, an American, was a self-taught painter. In 1826 Catlin saw a group of Indian chiefs visiting Philadelphia. He greatly admired them and decided then that his contribution to scientific knowledge would be to accurately paint Indians. In 1832 he traveled up the Missouri River by steamboat. His paintings of the western landscape along the Missouri were the first widely distributed views of the West. He stayed a month at Fort Union, 2000 miles (3220 km) up the Missouri. The Indians crowded around him, eager to have their portraits painted. His method of painting was to quickly outline the shape of the body and then to spend more time on the face, to make each Indian an individual. He usually completed his portraits in a studio back in the East, but only after he had made careful notes about the regalia, hairstyles, body paint, and weapons they carried. He realized that the daily lives of the Indians that he was capturing in his paintings were more important than the art itself. He took many trips to paint Indians, and by 1840 he wrote, "I have visited 48 tribes. . . I have brought home in good order, 310 portraits in oil, all painted in their native dress. . . and also 200 other paintings in oil containing views of their villages–their wigwams–their games and religious ceremonies–their dances–their ball plays–their buffalo hunting and other amusements; and the landscapes of the country they live in. . . ." His works were eventually donated to the Smithsonian Institution. Catlin also made three trips to Central and South America, seeking gold and painting the native cultures. He died in 1872, a true champion of native peoples.

In 1832 the German Prince Alexander Philipp Maximilian, accompanied by his hunter, David Dreidoppel, and the Swiss painter, Karl Bodmer, landed in the United States. He found the East Coast of the United States "too civilized" so he headed west hoping to see "wild America," especially the Indians. In 1833 the group traveled up the Missouri River and spent the winter with the Mandans. Bodmer's paintings of frontier America were first shown in a large exhibition in Paris in 1836. Since he was trained as an engraver, his paintings were very realistic and accurate. Many of the Indians he painted in 1833-34 died in a smallpox epidemic brought by white fur traders in 1837. The cultures and people he captured in his paintings would never be the same again.

Lewis' Return–Blackfoot Country Activity

Consider things in your life that you would like to remember. Think of things that may soon change if you don't draw or record them. Draw a detailed picture of one of these things. Include a detailed caption to go with your picture.

Clark's Return–Along the Yellowstone River

Lolo, Montana, to Below Little Knife River, North Dakota
July 3–August 12, 1806

Clark's group set off with fifty horses on July 3 to explore the southern route. He would head for Three Forks and split his group. Sergeant Ordway's group would canoe down the Missouri, following the same route they had used the summer before, and meet Lewis at the Marias River. Clark's group would continue on land, crossing to the Yellowstone River which they would follow to the Missouri River. (They did not find or explore what is today's Yellowstone National Park.)

Clark's group started along the beautiful valley of the Bitterroot River, filled with grasses and wildflowers. On July 4 Clark wrote, "This being the day of the decleration of Independence of the United States I had every disposition to selebrate and therefore halted early and partook of a Sumptious Dinner of a fat Saddle of Venison and Mush of Cows (roots)." They crossed the Continental Divide at today's Gibbon's Pass. Along Grasshopper Creek they camped directly on top of the one of the biggest goldfields ever discovered. If they had dug into the gravel, they would have become very rich. This was the later site of the gold-rush town, Bannack City, Montana.

On July 8 they reached the forks of the Jefferson River where they had sunk their canoes and cached supplies the previous August. The cache contained tobacco which the men had not had for many months. One canoe had a hole in it but was repaired. With the swift current it took only three days to get to Three Forks where the group divided. Sergeant Ordway and nine men paddled the canoes and most of the baggage to the Great Falls to meet Lewis' men. Clark, with ten men, Sacagawea, and Pomp, set out by land toward the Yellowstone River.

This was familiar country to Sacagawea. The Shoshones hunted here, and she had been here many times as a child. On July 13 Clark wrote, "I observe Several leading roads which appear to pass to a gap of the mountain. . . The indian woman who has been of great service to me as a pilot through this country recommends a gap in the mountain more south which I shall cross." They easily crossed this pass, later known as Bozeman Pass. The only hardship was suffered by the horses, whose hooves were sore and tender from the rocky ground. Clark solved this by having "Mockersons made of green (untanned) Buffalow Skin and put on their feet which seams to releve them very much."

Private Gibson had been bucked from his horse so horseback riding was painful. Clark decided that if they could find trees large enough for canoes, it would be a good place to start their river travel. On July 19 they stopped to look for trees and ". . . also hunt for some Wild Ginger for a Poltice for Gibsons wound." They found only small trees, so two narrow dugouts were made, but lashed together to make them more sturdy. That night, Crow Indians stole twenty-four of their fifty horses. (The captains felt that one disappointing gap in their expedition was that they had not actually met the Crows.) On July 24 most of the group set off by canoe. However, Sergeant Pryor took a small group overland with the remaining horses, hoping to trade them at the Mandan villages.

On July 25, Clark's canoe group stopped near today's Billings, Montana, to examine a sandstone tower. Clark wrote, "this rock I ascended and from its top had a most extensive view in every direction. This rock which I shall call Pompy's Tower is 200 feet high and 400 paces insecumpherance and only axcessable on one Side. The natives have ingraved on the face of this rock the figures of animals &c near which I marked my name and the day of the month & year." He named the rock after Sacagawea's baby. Today this is still known as Pompey's Pillar and Clark's signature has been preserved by the owners of this land.

On August 3 they reached the confluence of the Yellowstone and the Missouri where Clark had agreed to meet Lewis. However, the mosquitoes were so thick that they left the next day when they found that it was impossible to camp or hunt. They left a note for Lewis and went downriver to camp. On August 8 they were surprised to see Sergeant Pryor and his three men floating down the river toward them in two bullboats–round, bowl-shaped boats like those used by the Mandans. Indians had stolen the rest of the horses, so they made boats by stretching bison hides over frameworks made of young trees. Also, on the way to join Clark, a wolf had bitten Pryor's hand as he slept! Clark named a small river Pryor's River in honor of the sergeant who had tried so hard to carry out his orders. Three days later they met the two fur trappers Lewis would see the next day. From them they learned that the peace the captains had arranged between the Mandans and the Hidatsas with the Arikaras had not lasted long, and they were at war again. A few miles below the Little Knife River, on August 12, Lewis and Clark's groups met back together.

The Spelling Skills of William Clark

In the days of Lewis and Clark, spelling in the United States was not standardized. That means that it was acceptable to spell some words in a variety of ways. Most people did not have as much schooling as they do today so their spelling was not as good. There were not many books to teach them to spell. Noah Webster helped change this. When he was a teacher in Goshen, New York, in the 1780s, he wrote an elementary spelling book. Millions of copies of the speller were sold which helped standardize spellings and pronunciations. His famous dictionary, *An American Dictionary of the English Language*, was published in 1828.

As people read the journal of Captain William Clark, they are amused at some of his unusual spellings. It is said that Clark believed in freedom of spelling as well as other democratic freedoms, and he could spell as he chose! For the amount of education Clark had, he did very well writing his journal. What he recorded greatly expanded knowledge in the United States. His words *were* powerful. The spirit of adventure was stirred in people, forever changing the West.

Clark's Return–Along the Yellowstone River Activity

Don't be critical of Clark's writing, but have some fun "being Clark's teacher" and correcting the following journal entries:

1. Directly *on* his writing, make appropriate changes. Use proofreading symbols if they are familiar to you. Be sure you don't change the meaning of his writing. Sometimes there is more than one way a change can be made.
2. Then, on another paper, neatly rewrite the journal entry in a correct format.

July 24, 1806: When Clark camped near today's Billings, Montana, he had nice things to say about the area: "the earth which is rich is covered with wild rye and a Species of grass resembling the bluegrass, and a mixture of Sweet grass which the Indian plat and ware around their necks for its cent which is of a strong sent like that of the Vinella."

July 27, 1806: Near the confluence of the Big Horn and Yellowstone Rivers, game was plentiful. The bison were so noisy at night that the group's sleep was disturbed. The men would jump up at night in anger and fire their guns, trying to scare the animals away. Sometimes the group had to sit beside the river waiting for bison herds that were miles long to swim across the river ahead of them. There were also many elk and beaver.

"The Buffalow and Elk is estonishingly noumerous, particularly the Elk which are so jintle that we frequently pass within 20 or 30 paces of them without their being the least alarmd. when we pass the Big horn I take my leave of the View of the tremendious chain of Rocky Mountains white with Snow in View of which I have been since the 1st of May last."

August 3, 1806: The mosquitoes were so thick near the confluence of the Yellowstone and Missouri Rivers that Clark's group could not stand to wait there for Lewis' group. They moved farther down the Missouri River to camp and wait.

"last night the Musquetors was so troublesom that no one of the party Slept half the night. on the side of bluff I saw some of the Mountain Bighorn animals. I assended the hill below the Bluff. The Musquetors wer so noumerrous that I could not shute with any certainty and therefore soon returned to the Canoes."

Lewis and Clark, Reunited Along the Missouri

Below Little Knife River, North Dakota, to Above Sioux City, Iowa
August 12–September 2, 1806

On August 12, Lewis and Clark were happily reunited, after many adventures, almost on schedule, and without a loss of life! Clark was worried at first when he didn't see Lewis in the boats. He soon found him lying in the pirogue and learned of his gunshot wound. Clark found the wound was not life threatening. They left the two skin canoes and about three o'clock, set off together in the boats.

It took the group two more days to reach the Hidatsa and Mandan villages where they received a joyful reception. The river's edge was lined with crowds, and salutes of gunfire were exchanged. Clark scolded the chiefs for breaking the peace with the Arikaras. The Hidatsas and Mandans gave excuses, but they agreed to try again. Clark tried to convince the chiefs to travel with them to Washington, D.C. They were invited to ". . . visit their Great Father, the President of the U. States, and to hear his own counsels and receive his gifts. . . [and] protect and secure you from all your enemies. . . ." The Indians insisted that they would never pass through the Sioux lands alive. Finally, a Mandan chief, Sheheke (or Big White), agreed to make the trip if his wife and two children could also go.

John Colter had no desire to return to civilization and asked to be discharged from his army service. He wished to go back up the Missouri with fur traders who were excited about stories of the many beaver upriver and wanted Colter to be their guide. The captains felt that his good work on the trip had earned him the early release. They gave him some supplies and agreed to discharge him if no one else wanted the same privilege. (Colter was eventually the first white man to see the spectacular geysers and mudpots of today's Yellowstone National Park.)

Charbonneau was also paid off, since there would be no further interpreting duties for him or for Sacagawea. He was paid $500.33 which he used to buy a tent and a horse. Unlike her husband, Sacagawea received no pay for her help on the expedition. On August 17 Clark wrote, "we also took our leave of T. Chabono, his Snake Indian wife and their child who had accompanied us on our rout to the pacific ocean in the capacity of interpreter and interpretess. . . we offered to convey him down to the Illinois if he chose to go, he declind. . . observing that he had no acquaintance or prospects of makeing a liveing below, and must continue to live in the way he had done."

On August 17 the explorers fired a final salute from their rifles and set out down the Missouri toward home. Four days later they renewed friendships among the Arikaras. The Arikaras smoked with Big White, the Mandan chief, and agreed to be at peace again. On August 30 a number of Teton Sioux called to them from shore, but Clark lectured them, through an interpreter, on their bad conduct of two years before and refused to have anything more to do with them. Downriver they had a brief meeting with the friendly Yankton Sioux. This was their last significant meeting with Indians on the trip. Toward the end of August, Clark noted that "my worthy friend Capt. Lewis is recovering fast."

Lewis and Clark, Reunited Along the Missouri Activity

For about six weeks, Lewis and Clark took different routes on the return trip. They wanted to see as much of the land as possible. During their travels, they had many adventures and saw things that were new and amazing to them. When the two groups met back together along the Missouri River, below the confluence of the Little Knife River, they had much to share with each other.

Imagine that you could have listened in as Lewis and Clark sat around the evening campfire on August 12, 1806, and shared their experiences with each other. Record what they said, as if it were a script. Be sure to write in conversational format, using proper quotation marks, commas, and other punctuation.

Example:
"It was so hard to say good-bye to the Nez Perce guides. They left us on July 4 when they thought we were getting too close to the Hidatsa lands," said Lewis.

"They were such good friends," added Clark.

"Yes. We smoked the peace pipe and then the brother of Chief Cut Nose presented me with the gift of his own name, White Bearskin Folded," Lewis said.

"I know what an honor that is. I will never forget when Chief Cameahwait of the Shoshones presented me with his name," said Clark.

Here are some of the events Lewis and Clark experienced on their separate explorations. (You might wish to write about some of these, or you could do further research to get other ideas.)

Lewis
Saying good-bye to the Nez Perce
Crossing the Continental Divide on horses
Bison hunting
Opening flooded caches
Mosquito problems
McNeal's grizzly bear encounter
Exploring the Marias River
Evening with the Blackfeet Indians
Fighting the Blackfeet Indians
Escaping from the Blackfeet Indians
Canoeing down the Missouri
Finding Clark's note
Cruzatte shooting Lewis

Clark
Wildflowers along the Bitterroot River
Fourth of July dinner
Digging up caches/getting canoes from river
Canoeing downriver
Sacagawea helping find the route
Horses needing moccasins
Gibson bucked from horse
Making dugout canoes
Horses being stolen by Crow Indians
Writing on and naming Pompey's Pillar
Mosquito problems
Bullboats of Pryor
Pryor's wolf bite

End of the Journey–Return to St. Louis

Above Sioux City, Iowa, to St. Louis, Missouri
September 3–23, 1806

As Lewis and Clark paddled down the Missouri River, they began to meet people from whom they could learn what had been happening in the United States while they were gone. Clark wrote on September 3, "we Spied two boats & Several men. . . our first enquirey was after the President of our country and then our friends and the State of the politicks of our country. . . ."

On September 4 they stopped to visit Sergeant Floyd's grave. Clark wrote, "found the grave had been opened by the nativs and left half covered. we had this grave completely filled up, and returned to the canoes. . . ." As they began to enter the Ozarks region, Clark wrote on September 9, "the climate is every day preceptably wormer and air more Sultrey than I have experienced for a long time." He also wrote, "My worthy friend Cap Lewis has entirely recovered. . . can walk and run nearly as well as ever he could."

There were many trappers and traders going up the Missouri so Lewis and Clark were able to buy much-needed food which cut down hunting time. Some of the traders considered them as men "returned from the grave" because they were amazed that they were still alive and often gave them gifts of whiskey and food. On September 17 Clark wrote, "we met a Captain McClellin [who] informed us that we had been long Since given out by the people of the U.S. Generaly and almost forgotten, the President of the U. States had yet hopes of us." (He also wrote, "we saw cows on the bank which caused a shout to be raised for joy." They soon would not have to hunt for every meal.) One rumor had it that they had been eaten by wild animals, another that they had been killed by Indians, and a third that they had become slaves of the Spaniards. This made them even more eager to return home to prove the success of their mission.

On September 21 they reached St. Charles and "the party rejoiced at the Sight. . . ." They saluted the excited townspeople with three rounds from their guns. Clark wrote, "we rose early took the Chief to the publick store & furnished him with Some clothes &c."

They left the Missouri River on September 23 and headed down the Mississippi River to St. Louis. At noon they reached St. Louis and fired off their guns as a salute to the town. Clark wrote, "We were met by all the village and received a hearty welcome. . . ." The Lewis and Clark expedition was home again! They were eager to write letters to President Jefferson and their families and friends.

On the 25th the expedition was treated to a fancy dinner, complete with eighteen toasts, ending with "Captains Lewis and Clark–Their perilous services endear them to every American heart." The next day Clark made the final entry in his journal, "a fine morning. we commenced wrighting &c." Their trip had taken two years, four months, and nine days. They had covered 4134 miles (6656 km) from the mouth of the Missouri to the Pacific and 3555 miles (5724 km) back again. They had fought river currents, found trails over towering mountains, and met tribe after tribe of Indians, a successful journey of over 7500 miles (12,075 km)!

End of the Journey–Return to St. Louis Activity

Imagine that televisions existed at the time of Lewis and Clark. Also, imagine that you were either Lewis or Clark, just arriving back in St. Louis on September 23, 1806. It had been over two years since you left on your journey and most people had assumed you were dead or had forgotten all about you. The people of St. Louis were very excited when they heard you were returning. They lined the waterfront, cheering as you and the others paddled to the dock.

After one day of rest you were asked to appear as a guest on a morning television talk show, to answer questions about your journey. Write a script of this interview. List the questions asked and your responses. (Think carefully about what types of questions you would be asked.) Write this in proper conversation format. Put quotation marks around the actual words that were said.

Example:
Interviewer: "Mr. Lewis, we understand that the Mandan Indians tried to warn you about grizzly bears, but you didn't take them seriously. Is this true?"

M. Lewis: "That's true. We thought that the Indians had trouble with the grizzlies because they were trying to shoot them with bows and arrows. Since we were skilled riflemen, we were sure that the grizzlies would not be a great danger to us."

Interviewer: "Did it work out that way? Were the grizzly bears as much of a danger as the Mandans said?"

M. Lewis: "They were definitely dangerous! On May 14, about a month after we left the Mandans, we saw a grizzly lying in the open. Six of our hunters crept up on it. Four of them shot and hit it, but it started to attack. The other two shot and hit it, too, but the bear just kept coming. There was absolute panic!"

Interviewer: "How scary! What did you do?"

M. Lewis: "One of the men finally shot a bullet through its brain. By the time it finally died, it had been hit eight times, had a broken shoulder, and shots through both lungs. We certainly gained a new respect for grizzly bears!"

Results of the Lewis and Clark Expedition

As a result of their successful expedition, Lewis and Clark became the new heroes of the American West. Jefferson wrote of their return, "Never did a similar event excite more joy thro' the United States." There were newspaper reports, dinners, parties, parades, and speeches in their honor. The Lewis and Clark expedition gave Americans their first idea of what lay between the Mississippi River and the Pacific Ocean. President Jefferson was absolutely thrilled with the maps, specimens, and wealth of scientific and cultural knowledge that was gained.

Lewis and Clark's scientific discoveries were impressive. They encountered 24 Indian tribes and discovered 178 plants and 122 animals then unknown to science. Some of these included the pronghorn, bull snake, tern, prairie dog, jackrabbit, grouse, pelican, porcupine, and coyote. They even found the spine of what they thought had been a huge fish, and took along a few bones for Jefferson. The bones belonged not to a fish but to a prehistoric reptile. The reports they prepared for Jefferson were different from the reports of other explorers, who usually just looked for the best way to make quick profits. They did record information that would be helpful in the fur trade and made suggestions as to how the United States could get the better of the British. However, they also had written detailed descriptions of the customs and languages of the Indian tribes they had met.

After hearing the report of Lewis and Clark, one newspaper in New York suggested that the country they had explored was so wild that it would never be visited again! Some people could hardly believe the things the men said–bears that weighed a thousand pounds, mountains higher than the Adirondacks, a river bigger than the Missouri and so full of fish, trees taller than church steeples, and bison as far as the eye could see! Today, this wild land has been greatly changed. Lewis and Clark crossed mountains that had no highways and floated rivers that had no dams. Today, most of the prairie has been plowed or paved. Towns and cities are found throughout the West. Bison no longer roam the grasslands. The grizzly bear has almost disappeared, with only a few hundred still remaining. The great falls of the Missouri and the falls and rapids of the Columbia have been covered by power dams. A few areas look the way they did during the time of Lewis and Clark. The White Cliffs of the Missouri are protected by the Wild and Scenic Rivers law. Parts of the Rocky Mountains are preserved as wilderness areas. Some changes were positive and some negative, but few could probably have been imagined by Lewis and Clark!

The expedition had hoped to find what had been called the Northwest Passage, an easy water route across the North American continent so trade would be easier between the United States and China. They found that no water route existed and that a land route was longer and more difficult than had been previously imagined. Clark's maps were first published in 1814. The maps were used by government officials, the military, engineers, settlers, fur traders, schools, and explorers. The captains' survey work helped give the United States a solid claim to the Oregon Country. The successful completion of the trip started people thinking that perhaps the United States could extend all the way from the Atlantic to the Pacific. When Patrick Gass, the expedition's last white survivor, died at age 99 in 1870, the continental limits of the United States stood where they are today. If their expedition had not been successful, Americans who live between the Rockies and Pacific might be Canadian or British citizens today.

The Lewis and Clark expedition was the first group of Americans to cross the North American continent and the first group of white men to reach the Pacific by way of the Missouri-Columbia route. (Alexander Mackenzie, a British-Canadian explorer, had led an expedition across the Continental Divide in 1793.) Word spread quickly of the rich beaver country that had been found. Lewis wrote to Jefferson in September 1806, after their return, "That portion of the Continent watered by the Missouri and all its branches from the Cheyenne upwards is richer in beaver and otter than any country on earth. . . ." Fur trappers and traders started up the Missouri River. Men's stovepipe top hats, made from beaver pelts, were the fashion of the day. A lot of money could be made by trapping and selling the pelts. Until the fashion changed in the 1840s, the impact of the fur trappers was great.

Others soon followed–frontier soldiers, missionaries, businessmen, farmers, ranchers, gold miners, and families following the westward trails. The expedition had found rich new land. They had told Jefferson that the land in Oregon was not only rich in furs but would make good farmland. The Oregon Trail went directly across the plains and over the mountains to the south of the Lewis and Clark route. Lewis and Clark were the first to show it was possible. The first large wagon train over the Oregon Trail was in 1843. Gold was discovered in California in 1848, and the prospectors then started out, eventually mining in many regions throughout the West. By 1869, a railroad to California had been completed.

Jefferson had wanted Lewis and Clark to establish friendly relations with the Indian tribes they met. They were fairly successful in this, but the friendships between the Indians and white men did not last. They began to collapse as more and more hunters, trappers, and settlers moved in on the Indians' lands. At the same time, Indian populations were being devastated by diseases new to them such as smallpox and alcoholism. The opening of the West was a mixed blessing. For the Indians, it did much more harm than good. The Yakima Nation Heritage Center at Toppenish, Washington, has a drawing of the Yakimas meeting Lewis and Clark in 1805. The sign by the drawing reads, "One day downriver from the East came strangers, white men and a black man in canoes. We received them as honored guests, as tradition would have us do. In a few days they departed downstream to the West. Life for our people would never be the same."

Results of the Lewis and Clark Expedition Activity

Make a time line of events to help understand the history of West in the eighty-four years after the travels of Lewis and Clark. Events and dates are listed in a scrambled order. Decide which dates go with which events. Then form them into a time line. Other events may be added too. You might also wish to make a time line of the Lewis and Clark expedition, as shown in this example:

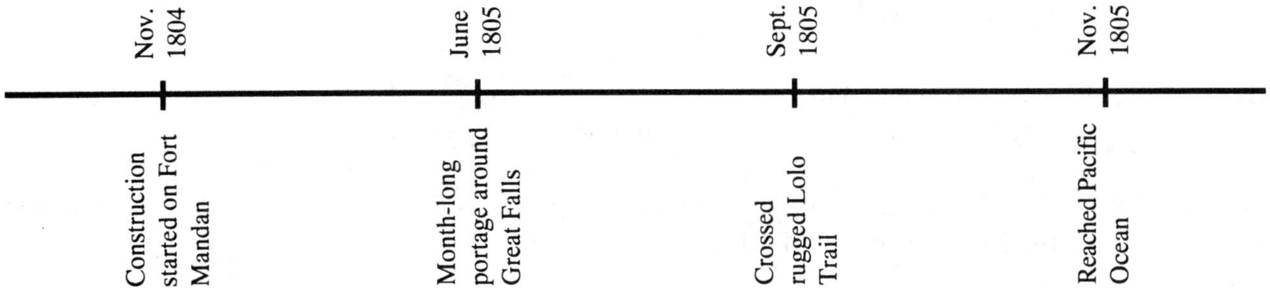

Sept. 23, 1806 End of the Civil War. Confederate General Robert E. Lee surrendered at Appomattox Court House, Virginia.

Sept. 8, 1810 Alaska Purchase Treaty transferred Alaska to the United States from Russia for $7,200,000.

June 19, 1812 The first of 1000 pioneers left Missouri, bound for Oregon, starting emigration on the Oregon Trail.

Feb. 17, 1820 First transcontinental telegraph line was linked up and the first message was sent between San Francisco and Washington, D.C. (Pony Express now not needed.)

Apr. 17, 1824 The Butterfield Overland Mail Company started its first run from St. Louis to San Francisco, which covered the 3000 miles (4830 km) in just under twenty-four days.

Mar. 3, 1825 Congress authorized a survey to mark the Santa Fe Trail between the Missouri River and New Mexico.

Apr. 10, 1830 President Lincoln died after being shot by an assassin the previous evening. Andrew Johnson became President.

June 30, 1834 President Grant signed an act of Congress creating Yellowstone National Park in Wyoming Territory.

Sept. 12, 1836 Congress agreed to set the Oregon-British boundary at the 49th parallel, ending co-ownership of the Oregon territory.

May 22, 1843 President Madison declared war on Great Britain, which became known as the War of 1812. (Ended Dec. 24, 1814)

June 15, 1846 Congress established a Department of Indian Affairs, but it stayed under the War Department until 1849.

Jan. 24, 1848 Gold was discovered at Sutter's Creek near Sacramento, California, which started the Gold Rush.

Feb. 2, 1848 President Polk signed the Oregon Bill, establishing the Oregon Territory.

Aug. 14, 1848 The Senate passed the Missouri Compromise Measure, bringing Missouri into the U.S. as a slave state and Maine as a free state. There could be no slavery north of latitude 36 30'.

Sept. 16, 1858 The first run of the Pony Express left St. Joseph, Missouri, for Sacramento, California. It took the relay riders ten days to carry the mail.

Apr. 3, 1860 A U.S.-Russia treaty was signed saying the southern limit of the Russian claim in the Northwest was 54 40'.

Nov. 6, 1860 The last major battle between Indians and the U.S. Army was fought at Wounded Knee Creek, South Dakota.

Apr. 12, 1860 Dr. Marcus Whitman reached Fort Vancouver and soon set up a mission near today's Walla Walla, Washington. His wife, Narcissa, and friend, Eliza Spaulding, were the first white women to cross the North American continent.

Oct. 24, 1861 The Lewis and Clark expedition returned to St. Louis.

Apr. 9, 1865 The start of John Jacob Astor's fur-trading business. He sent a ship, the *Tonquin,* from New York to Oregon.

Apr. 15, 1865 First U.S. transcontinental railroad was completed at Promontory Point in Utah Territory.

Mar. 30, 1867 The Civil War began when Confederate forces fired on Fort Sumter in Charleston Harbor, South Carolina.

May 10, 1869 Abraham Lincoln was elected President of the United States.

Mar. 1, 1872 William Sublette led ten wagons out of St. Louis to Wind River, Wyoming, to the annual fur rendezvous, the first wagons to travel on the Oregon Trail. The ease of travel showed that wagons could cross the continent.

Dec. 29, 1890 The U.S. and Mexico signed the Treaty of Guadalupe Hidalgo, ending the Mexican-American War. The U.S. got the territories of New Mexico, California, and the Rio Grande border of Texas.

The Permanent Party
Appendix I

In Command
Captain Meriwether Lewis, First U.S. Infantry
Second Lieutenant (his official rank) William Clark, U.S. Corps of Artillerists

Sergeants
John Ordway
Nathaniel Pryor
Charles Floyd (died August 20, 1804)
Patrick Gass (replaced Floyd, August 26, 1804)

Privates
William Bratton
John Collins
John Colter
Pierre (Peter) Cruzatte
Joseph Field(s)
Reuben Field(s)
Robert Frazer (enlisted October 8, 1804, at the Arikara villages)
George Gibson
Silas Goodrich
Hugh Hall
Thomas P. Howard
Francois (Francis) Labiche
Baptiste Lepage (enlisted November 2, 1804, at the Mandan villages)
Hugh McNeal
John Newman (dropped from the permanent party October 13, 1804, and later discharged at the Mandan villages)
John Potts
Moses B. Reed (deserted August 4, 1804, captured and discharged)
George Shannon
John Shields
John B. Thompson
William Werner
Joseph Whitehouse
Alexander H. Williard
Richard Windsor
Peter M. Wiser

Interpreters
George Drouillard (generally spelled Drewyer in the journals)
Toussiant Charbonneau

Other Members
York, Clark's slave
Sacagawea, Charbonneau's Shoshone wife
Jean Baptiste Charbonneau (Pomp), their child
Seaman, Lewis' Newfoundland dog

Bibliography

Books, Magazines, Pamphlets

America's Fascinating Indian Heritage edited by James A. Maxwell. Pleasantville, NY: The Reader's Digest Association, Inc., 1990. This reference book describes the customs, art, history, and way of life of Native Americans from ten regions throughout the United States and Canada. There are detailed text and colorful drawings and photographs.

Bold Journey–West with Lewis and Clark by Charles Bohner. Boston, MA: Houghton Mifflin Company, 1985. This children's novel imagines what part Private Hugh McNeal might have played on the journey. His name is listed among the members of the permanent party but little is known of him.

Call Him a Good Old Dog, but Don't Call Him Scannon by Donald Jackson. Portland, OR: Reprinted from the July 1985 issue of *We Proceeded On*, the official publication of the Lewis and Clark Trail Heritage Foundation, Inc., WPO Publication No. 2A, March 1986. Detailed pamphlet explaining the handwriting mix-up in the name of Lewis' Newfoundland dog, from Scannon to the correct name of Seaman.

Fort Clatsop–The Story Behind the Scenery by Daniel J. Dattilio, interpretive specialist for the National Park Service. Las Vegas, NV: KC Publications, 1986. Booklet of colorful photography describing life at Fort Clatsop during the winter of 1805-06.

The Journals of Lewis and Clark edited by Bernard DeVoto. Boston, MA: Houghton Mifflin Company, 1953. Condensation of the journals of Lewis and Clark, slightly shortened and edited for the general reader, yet maintaining the spirit, accuracy, and spellings of the original journals. It also includes three appendices: Jefferson's instructions to Lewis, personnel of the expedition, and itemized specimens and artifacts sent to Jefferson from Fort Mandan.

Lewis and Clark and the Route to the Pacific by Seamus Cavan. New York, NY: Chelsea House Publishers, 1991. This book chronologically describes the journey of Lewis and Clark. It is written for the general reader, illustrated with paintings from the time of the expedition.

Lewis and Clark Country, text by Archie Satterfield and photography by David Muench. Portland, Oregon: Beautiful America Publishing Company, 1978. The text chronologically describes the journey of Lewis and Clark. The text is supplemented by gorgeous full-page photographs of what the countryside must have looked like during the days of the expedition.

The Lewis and Clark Expedition by Patrick McGrath. Morristown, NJ: Silver Burdett Company, 1985. Chronological overview of the journal, especially for children. Story of the journey, with colorful pictures and additional information on food in the wilderness, the language barrier, and tribes along the way.

The Lewis and Clark Expedition 1804-1806 edited by Frances Nankin. Peterborough, NH: Cobblestone Publishing, Inc., 1980. This issue of *Cobblestone Magazine* is devoted entirely to the Lewis and Clark expedition. Biographical information is given on Lewis, Clark, Sacagawea, Jefferson, York, and Seaman.

Lewis and Clark Trail by Gerald W. Olmsted. New York, NY: Fielding Travel Books, 1986. This book is described as a "reliving history guide," describing in detail each part of the journey. The expedition is described, including journal quotations, how to find the trail today, tourist information about each area, and detailed maps.

Lewis and Clark–Voyage of Discovery by Dan Murphy. Las Vegas, NV: KC Publications, 1977. This booklet chronologically describes the journey of Lewis and Clark. It is highlighted by photographs by David Muench, plus journal quotations, and a map with each section showing the progress of the trip.

Our Dog Scannon–Partner in Discovery by Ernest Staples Osgood. Portland, OR: a supplemental publication of We Proceeded On, the official publication of the Lewis and Clark Trail Heritage Foundation, Inc., WPO Publication No. 2, July 1977. Detailed pamphlet telling about Lewis' Newfoundland dog, Seaman (the correct name had not been determined at the time of publication of this pamphlet). This includes journal references plus information on the Newfoundland breed.

Streams to the River, River to the Sea by Scott O'Dell. Boston, MA: Houghton Mifflin Company, 1986. This children's novel about Sacagawea won the Hans Christian Andersen Award. The story tells of the Lewis and Clark expedition through the eyes of Sacagawea.

To the Pacific with Lewis and Clark by Ralph K. Andrist and the editors of American Heritage (American Heritage Junior Library). Mahwah, NJ: Troll Associates, 1967. This is a very complete book, especially for children but detailed enough for adults as well, chronologically describing the journey of Lewis and Clark. It contains artwork, photographs, maps, journal quotations, and general information.

The Way to the Western Sea–Lewis and Clark Across the Continent by David Lavender. New York, NY: Doubleday, 1988. This is a very detailed reference book, chronologically describing the expedition. There are three appendices telling of Jefferson's instructions to Lewis, the names of the permanent party, and additional information about the ship the *Lydia*.

The West of the Imagination by William H. and William N. Goetzmann. New York, NY: W.W. Norton & Company, 1986. This detailed reference book shows the West through the eyes of the artists who captured these scenes from history. A few of the many artists include George Catlin, Frederic Remington, Charles Russell, William H. Jackson, and Karl Bodmer.

West to the Pacific–The Story of the Lewis and Clark Expedition by Ronald K. Fisher. Coeur d'Alene, ID: Alpha Omega, 1989. This book chronologically describes the Lewis and Clark expedition. The information is detailed enough for adults but could be read by students. Pen and ink drawings add to the text.

The World Almanac of the American West edited by John S. Bowman. New York, NY: Pharos Books, 1986. History of the American West is described from August 3, 1492, through August 19, 1985. The text is written like a calendar. Each event is described in a paragraph. An event that covers more than one day will usually be found updated on many dates. Events are labeled under categories of exploration, international, discovery, commerce, westward movement, settling, arts/culture, Indians, missionary work, war, life/customs, finance, transportation, mining, national, science/technology, industry, conservation, education, and the like.